TRANSPORTATION
FOR CITIES

TRANSPORTATION FOR CITIES
The Role of Federal Policy

WILFRED OWEN

THE BROOKINGS INSTITUTION
Washington, D.C.

Copyright © 1976 by
THE BROOKINGS INSTITUTION
1775 Massachusetts Avenue, N.W., Washington, D.C. 20036

Library of Congress Cataloging in Publication Data:

Owen, Wilfred.
    Transportation for cities.

    Includes bibliographical references.
    1. Urban transportation policy–United States.
2. Federal aid to transportation–United States.
3. Transportation and state–United States.   I. Title.
HE308.09   388.4'0973   75-44508
ISBN 0-8157-6773-0

9 8 7 6 5 4 3 2 1

THE BROOKINGS INSTITUTION is an independent organization devoted to nonpartisan research, education, and publication in economics, government, foreign policy, and the social sciences generally. Its principal purposes are to aid in the development of sound public policies and to promote public understanding of issues of national importance.

The Institution was founded on December 8, 1927, to merge the activities of the Institute for Government Research, founded in 1916, the Institute of Economics, founded in 1922, and the Robert Brookings Graduate School of Economics and Government, founded in 1924.

The Board of Trustees is responsible for the general administration of the Institution, while the immediate direction of the policies, program, and staff is vested in the President, assisted by an advisory committee of the officers and staff. The bylaws of the Institution state: "It is the function of the Trustees to make possible the conduct of scientific research, and publication, under the most favorable conditions, and to safeguard the independence of the research staff in the pursuit of their studies and in the publication of the results of such studies. It is not a part of their function to determine, control, or influence the conduct of particular investigations or the conclusions reached."

The President bears final responsibility for the decision to publish a manuscript as a Brookings book. In reaching his judgment on the competence, accuracy, and objectivity of each study, the President is advised by the director of the appropriate research program and weighs the views of a panel of expert outside readers who report to him in confidence on the quality of the work. Publication of a work signifies that it is deemed a competent treatment worthy of public consideration but does not imply endorsement of conclusions or recommendations.

The Institution maintains its position of neutrality on issues of public policy in order to safeguard the intellectual freedom of the staff. Hence interpretations or conclusions in Brookings publications should be understood to be solely those of the authors and should not be attributed to the Institution, to its trustees, officers, or other staff members, or to the organizations that support its research.

Foreword

For many years federal policy governing the allocation of aid for transportation reflected little understanding of urban needs or ignored them altogether. As automobile ownership increased in the United States, the lion's share of available funds went to rural highways. Urban roads were eligible for aid only if they could facilitate intercity movement as extensions of the interstate network. Public transit received no federal assistance at all until as recently as 1964, when the effects of U.S. transportation policy on an urbanized society made such aid a compelling need.

Today seven out of every ten Americans live in urban areas and are finding the interrelated problems of transportation, energy, and the environment increasingly relevant to their daily lives. Fortunately, these problems—manifested in automobile congestion, pollution, the uncertain outlook for fuel, and poor public transit—have been prompting new and more discriminating federal transportation policies. Recent legislation emphasizes aid to public transit through a program that has grown from a $30 million effort to a multibillion-dollar one, and local governments can now shift a substantial portion of road money to bus and rail alternatives.

In this study Wilfred Owen expands the transportation analysis he presented in his 1972 Brookings book, *The Accessible City,* by examining the merits and shortcomings of recent federal programs to improve mobility in the metropolis. Improvement, he emphasizes, requires not only more effective transportation systems, but also a halt to the decay of cities and the sprawl of suburbs—conditions that force people to use transportation for escape and as a means of compensating for the inaccessibility of jobs, housing, shopping centers, and recreation. In the belief that such conditions made desirable a program coordinating environmental influences, energy conservation, and transportation, he suggests alternative approaches to the improvement of urban mobility and compares their costs and benefits.

Mr. Owen is a senior fellow in the Brookings Economic Studies program. His research for this project was supported principally by grants from Carnegie Corporation of New York and the Richard King Mellon Foundation.

The author wishes to acknowledge the assistance of the U.S. Department of Transportation in making data available for the study. His special thanks go to Alice M. Rivlin for reviewing the manuscript before leaving Brookings to head the Congressional Budget Office. Valuable help was also provided by Robert Dorfman of Harvard University; by Robert W. Hartman of Brookings; by Robert D. Reischauer of the Congressional Budget Office; and by the members of the manuscript review committee, Alan Altshuler of the Massachusetts Institute of Technology, C. Kenneth Orski of the Urban Mass Transportation Administration, and Leon M. Cole of the Congressional Research Service of the Library of Congress.

The author is also indebted to Evelyn P. Fisher for verifying the statistical material, to Tadd Fisher for editing the manuscript, to Thang Long Ton That for research assistance, and to Margaret H. Su for secretarial services.

The views expressed in the study are those of the author and should not be attributed to any of the persons whose assistance is acknowledged above, to Carnegie Corporation of New York, to the Richard King Mellon Foundation, or to the trustees, officers, or staff members of the Brookings Institution.

GILBERT Y. STEINER
Acting President

Washington, D.C.
February 1976

Contents

Tables

Introduction

In recent years the federal government has initiated extraordinary measures to assist the cities with their transportation problems. These measures are bound to have far-reaching effects on the future of urban America—not simply on how people move but on how they live.

The current program is a sharp departure from conventional federal aid for transportation, which for many years ignored the cities and later made billions of dollars available for roads and ignored public transit. Today's multibillion-dollar annual effort to aid urban transportation could hardly have been anticipated a few years ago. In 1964 federal assistance in support of public transit totaled a modest $30 million; by 1975 it had reached an annual level of $1.4 billion. Current legislation increases this amount, establishes the first long-term federal commitment to transit, and provides not only for capital investments but for transit operating subsidies as well. These provisions have been accompanied by changes in federal aid for highways that greatly expand the federal program in urban areas and permit local governments to shift substantial amounts of road money to bus and rail alternatives. Total federal assistance for urban transportation is now approaching $5 billion a year, with no end in sight.

The new programs are the nation's response to the very real problems of traffic congestion and pollution that are plaguing the cities. These problems include the mounting social costs of an automobile-dominated environment, the disruptive effects of expressways on urban communities, the widespread public opposition to the acquisition of more land for highways, the precipitous decline of public transit service, the disadvantages suffered by people without cars, and the current fears of a motorized society about its dependence on foreign petroleum to keep the metropolis moving.

Under the program to resurrect public transit thousands of buses are being purchased, extensive rapid transit investments are being made in the larger metropolitan areas, and beginning in 1975 transit operating deficits can be covered in part with federal funds. But urban mobility is not exclusively a matter of money or of hardware. Supplying good transportation in urban areas also involves the way the total system is operated, including the automobile as well as transit. There is an urgent need for better regulation of traffic, for more effective pricing and tax policies, and for the design and production of energy-efficient cars.

Both city and suburb are heavily dependent on the private automobile, and beyond a certain point conventional public transit will be unable to provide a practical substitute. The task is not simply to expand public transportation but to assure the continuation of private transportation. It would be ironic if the effort to correct the overemphasis on highways should lead to an overemphasis on transit, repeating the old mistakes with a new technology.

Because of the importance of the automobile to urban transportation, there is a vital need to link energy policy to federal transportation policy. Higher prices for petroleum or the alternative of rationing to reduce fuel consumption should be related to positive approaches to achieving more energy-efficient movement, including a rapid changeover to a new type of automobile and the introduction of public transit alternatives that can provide more attractive substitutes for the automobile. At the same time, a reduction in the volume of unnecessary transportation could be accomplished through changes in the conditions that generate travel demand. Changing the environment and the location of jobs and housing may save as much energy as riding the bus.

The magnitude of the requirements projected for urban transportation emphasizes the importance of examining public policy more closely. Highway and transit investments projected by the states in a federally sponsored survey establish urban transportation capital needs for the period 1970-90 at one-third of a trillion dollars (1969 prices).[1] It is not clear whether this enormous outlay will actually help the cities or whether the physical disruptions and financial burdens imposed by such a program will hasten their decline.

In seeking solutions to urban transportation problems, policymakers should take into account the following considerations:

—The extent to which urban Americans depend on the automobile and the relation of automobile dependency to trends in the location of people and jobs.

—The measures necessary to create a public transportation capability that will serve urban areas effectively.

1. U.S. Department of Transportation, "1972 National Transportation Report" (DOT, 1972; processed), pp. 3-28, 3-29.

—The nature of federal policies, their contribution to current unsatisfactory transportation conditions, and the ways in which policy reform might bring about a more equitable situation for both car owners and those without cars.

—The possibilities of more radical longer-range transportation solutions through a combination of new technology and efforts to design a more satisfying urban environment.

—The new dimensions of the urban transportation problem that have been introduced by uncertainties about the energy supply.

—The cost implications for the public and private sectors of alternative approaches to urban transport solutions.

1

Moving in the Metropolis

An outstanding characteristic of American cities is their dependence on the automobile. Over 100 million passenger cars in the United States account for about eight out of every ten vehicle miles traveled, and more than half the driving is concentrated in urban areas where seven out of ten Americans live. Since 1960 the number of automobiles on the highways has increased by 44 million, and in some cities the volume of automobile commuter traffic has doubled in a decade. The decline in public transit has been nearly as spectacular. Transit lines are carrying 8 billion fewer passengers than in 1950 (table 1-1) —a 60 percent decrease in patronage—and 200 communities have abandoned public transportation services altogether. From a condition of moderate prosperity in the early sixties, the industry has fallen deep into the red, with operating deficits of more than $1 billion a year and costs still rising.[1]

1. Data on automobiles and commuter traffic are from Motor Vehicle Manufacturers Association of the U.S., *1975 Automobile Facts and Figures* (Detroit: MVMA, n.d.), pp. 16, 46; and American Institute of Planners (AIP) and MVMA, *Urban Transportation Factbook* (Detroit: MVMA, 1974), p. I-55. For data on urban population, see U.S. Bureau of the Census, *Statistical Abstract of the United States, 1974* (Government Printing Office, 1974), p. 19. For transit statistics, see American Public Transit Association, *'74-'75 Transit Fact Book* (Washington, D.C.: APTA, 1975), pp. 12, 17; and George W. Hilton, *Federal Transit Subsidies: The Urban Mass Transportation Assistance Program* (American Enterprise Institute for Public Policy Research, 1974), p. 3.

Much of the data in this chapter is from the *Urban Transportation Factbook*, a comprehensive analysis of urban travel in relation to population and employment that is based on the findings of the 1970 census. In most cases, it represents the latest available data of this kind. Since new data are limited and not always comparable with those of the census, updating has not been possible in certain sections of the chapter. The census information, however, remains relevant today.

Table 1-1. Trend in Transit Revenue Passengers, Selected Years, 1940-74

Billions

Year	Streetcar	Rapid transit	Bus	Total revenue passengers[a]
1940	4.2	2.3	3.6	10.5
1945	7.1	2.6	8.3	19.0
1950	2.8	2.1	7.7	13.8
1955	0.8	1.7	5.7	9.2
1960	0.3	1.7	5.1	7.5
1965	0.2	1.7	4.7	6.8
1970	0.2	1.6	4.1	5.9
1974	0.1	1.4	4.0	5.6

Source: American Public Transit Association, *'74-'75 Transit Fact Book* (Washington, D.C.: APTA, 1975), p. 17.
a. Total includes trolleybus.

Dependence on the Automobile

Eighty percent of all households in the United States have at least one car, 30 percent have two or more, and people spend about twice as much each year just to register their cars as they do to ride buses and subways.[2] For the nation as a whole, consumer outlays for cars and their operation in 1973 totaled $103 billion; for transit, the consumer expenditure was $1.6 billion.[3]

Cars, like people, are heavily concentrated in metropolitan areas. Urban areas with more than a million automobiles include Cleveland, St. Louis, Pittsburgh, San Francisco, and Washington. Detroit, New York, and Philadelphia each have approximately 2 million cars, while Los Angeles has 3.8 million. The ratio of people to cars in most big metropolitan areas (New York excepted) is 2 to 1.[4] The dominance of the automobile in urban areas is reflected in the estimate that 87 percent of all rides taken in U.S. cities are automobile trips.[5]

The reason for preferring private over public transit is not, as often alleged, the perversity of the consumer or his ignorance of economics. Part of the reason can be ascribed to public policy that has favored the car, but the basic reason why most urban trips are made by automobile is that the family car,

2. MVMA, *1975 Automobile Facts and Figures*, pp. 32, 65; and APTA, *'74-'75 Transit Fact Book*, p. 19.
3. U.S. Department of Commerce, *Survey of Current Business*, vol. 54 (July 1974), p. 24.
4. MVMA, *1975 Automobile Facts and Figures*, p. 23.
5. U.S. Department of Transportation, "1974 National Transportation Report" (Government Printing Office, 1974; processed), p. IV-1.

despite its shortcomings, is superior to any other method of transportation. It offers comfort, privacy, limited walking, minimum waiting, and freedom from schedules or routing. It guarantees a seat; protects the traveler from heat, cold, and rain; provides space for baggage; carries extra passengers at no extra cost; and for most trips, except those in the center city, gets there faster and cheaper than any other way. The transit rider confronts an entirely different situation. He must walk, wait, stand, and be exposed to the elements. The ride is apt to be costly, slow, and uncomfortable because of antiquated equipment, poor ventilation, and service that is congested in rush hours, infrequent during any other time of day, inoperative at night, and nonexistent in suburbia.

The automobile is also a highly versatile method of movement that serves commuter, social, recreational, and business travel needs alike. On a nationwide basis about one-third of all auto travel is accounted for by the trip to work. Another third is for educational, social, and recreational use. The remaining third is for family business, such as shopping, going to the doctor, and serving as chauffeur to the children. Most trips are short—half of them less than five miles one way.

It is easy to make a choice between car and public carrier on the basis of the service rendered and the costs that have to be paid. On a service basis the automobile generally wins out on time savings alone. Automobile drivers that travel ten miles to work average 24 minutes commuting time; transit riders average 50 minutes. The average travel time for the work trip is 21 minutes for the motorist and 37 minutes for the transit rider.[6] When it comes to cost, the amount that people pay to drive depends on whether their car is large or small, new or used. The average total cost to the consumer of operating a standard automobile in 1973 was about 16 cents a mile; driving a compact car cost 13 cents a mile.[7] But in urban areas vehicle operating costs increase with stop-and-go driving, and the marginal cost of highways for heavy-density commuter traffic is also substantial. In a study completed in 1973, the full economic cost of urban driving was estimated at something over 26 cents a mile, rapid transit cost 25 cents a mile, and bus 8 to 9 cents a mile.[8] Costs for urban driving are now about 15 percent higher due to increases in the price

6. U.S. Department of Transportation, Federal Highway Administration, "Nationwide Personal Transportation Study," Report 8 (DOT: 1973; processed), p. 32.

7. L. L. Liston and R. W. Sherrer, "Cost of Operating an Automobile" (U.S. Department of Transportation, Federal Highway Administration, 1974; processed), pp. 9, 10.

8. Marshall F. Reed, Jr., "Comparison of Urban Travel Economic Costs" (Washington, D.C.: Highway Users Federation, 1973; processed), p. A-20. Estimates are based on a limited sample; rapid transit figures are based on the Washington Metro system, now under construction.

of gasoline that began in 1974, and rising costs have resulted in an upward trend in transit fares.[9]

But the figures conceal some inherent financial advantages the urban motorist enjoys and the transit user does not. The former is not obliged to pay outright for any given trip, and extra passengers ride at no extra cost. The marginal operating cost for any given auto trip, mostly for gasoline, may be only 4 or 5 cents a mile, and to a driver making a short trip the perceived cost may be zero. But even if total costs (exclusive of parking) are taken into account, a short trip by automobile will almost always be well below the fare that would have to be paid to ride the bus, for bus fares are generally based on average costs for all riders and not on the specific trip being taken. Another significant difference between public and private transportation costs is the payment made to the driver. The motorist supplies his own free labor, whereas a major cost item for bus operations is driver wages.

As a means of providing transportation in cities, however, the automobile has its drawbacks. The most obvious are the demands it makes on limited urban space. In central cities a large proportion of the available land area is devoted to streets, highways, and parking, and this dedication of real estate to the movement and storage of vehicles has disrupted neighborhoods and damaged the environment. The result has been that cities have become a combination of traffic way and parking lot, with the emphasis on moving rather than on pleasant living conditions. The unwanted side effects of the automobile include noise, polluted air, polluted roadsides, and death or injury for tens of thousands of people annually.

The automobile in addition has become a source of inequity for city dwellers who do not drive—those who are too young or too old, the disabled, and those with low incomes. Close to 55 percent of households getting less than $3,000 a year have no car, and 32 percent of households with incomes of $3,000 to $4,999 are without cars.[10] But the spatial arrangements of the city have been developed on the assumption that everyone drives. Stores are remote from housing, housing remote from jobs, and in large areas of the metropolis almost every requirement of daily living depends on having a car. For those who do not drive, therefore, many of the opportunities for work and for enjoying the benefits supposedly made available by urban living are foreclosed.

The automobile is also a voracious consumer of materials and energy. It uses 20 percent of the nation's steel, 47 percent of its malleable iron, 33 per-

9. See APTA, *'74-'75 Transit Fact Book*, p. 20.
10. MVMA, *1975 Automobile Facts and Figures*, p. 32.

cent of its zinc, and over 60 percent of annual rubber supplies. It is a major user of glass, textiles, electrical equipment, plastics, and chemicals. Every year the United States scraps more cars than all the automobiles operating in South America. Four out of five vehicles scrapped are now entering the collection and recycling system, however, and the materials drain has lessened as the price of metals has encouraged the fuller recovery of abandoned cars.[11]

Uncertainty about the supply and price of energy is a major new resource problem affecting the future of the automobile. The U.S. transportation system accounts for 25 percent of the nation's total energy consumption and for 53 percent of its petroleum consumption. Passenger travel by automobile is responsible for somewhat more than half of the petroleum used for transport.[12]

The demand for fuel has increased steadily until very recently owing to several factors. First, the number of cars has doubled in the past two decades.[13] Second, until the current uncertainty about fuel supplies caused U.S. manufacturers to have second thoughts about car design, they continued to increase the weight and power of the average passenger car. These powerful cars, driven at the higher speeds permitted on interstate highways, were operated at sharply lower levels of gasoline efficiency until the federally imposed 55-mile speed limit in 1974. Third, automatic transmissions, antipollution devices, and air conditioning have all added to fuel consumption.

The energy efficiency of the automobile generally compares unfavorably with other methods of travel. In rush hours, a bus carrying 42 people gets about nine times as many passenger miles to a gallon of fuel as a standard automobile with the driver riding alone.[14] The trouble is, however, that buses (and subways) that are poorly patronized are also energy inefficient. The efficiency of different methods of transportation varies not only with the technology but with the load. A subway that is little used in off-peak hours may be highly inefficient in passenger miles generated per unit of energy, and a small car with four passengers is more energy efficient than a bus under any circumstances. What is needed, therefore, is a system of transportation that incorporates a mix of vehicles that are used in ways that take advantage of their inherent efficiencies. An appropriate combination of public and private transportation technologies is needed to supply the resource-conserving mobility required in urban areas. The federal aid program for

11. Ibid., pp. 26, 30, 53, 59.
12. Highway Users Federation, *Reporter*, January 1975, p. 4.
13. MVMA, *1975 Automobile Facts and Figures*, p. 24.
14. Richard A. Rice, "Historical Perspective in Transport System Development," in Mary Anne Williamson, ed., *Advanced Urban Transportation Systems* (Carnegie-Mellon University, Transportation Research Institute, 1970), p. 89.

urban transportation provides the means of accomplishing such a desirable transportation mix.

The Public Transit Alternative

Federal interest in better public transit that began with a concern about congestion and air pollution has been intensified by increasing public opposition to expressways. It has also been strengthened by the fact that the automobile, as a major consumer of petroleum, leaves the city vulnerable to a supply cutoff; hence the effort to de-emphasize the private car and to revive the sagging transit alternative. The question is to what extent public transit services can be expanded to absorb part of the trip-taking accommodated by automobiles and how best to go about it.

The transit rider has been the victim of an economic and political climate different from that enjoyed by the motorist. He is often poor, old, or otherwise disadvantaged, and there are no transit lobbies equal in power to those that champion the needs of the motorist. As a result the equipment used to provide public transportation has typically been overaged, the service poor, and even basic information about routes and schedules hard to come by. Furthermore, since most transit companies were in the private sector until recently, they not only were attempting to cover full costs through fares but to make a profit as well. But regulatory bodies often refused to grant needed fare increases, and this resulted in a shortage of capital to buy new equipment and in a further deterioriation of service.

Thus the consumer has regarded public transit as a last resort. The high point of 19 billion riders a year was reached during World War II, when automobile production ceased and gasoline was strictly rationed. Since then the streetcar has all but disappeared, many bus lines have been discontinued, most riders have defected to the automobile, and despite the very large gains in urban population, transit riding in 1973 commanded only 0.2 percent of consumer expenditures.[15] The number of transit rides in 1974—5.6 billion—was close to the lowest number recorded since the turn of the century (see table 1-1).

The result is apparent in the changes that occurred in the methods of urban travel between 1960 and 1970. During that period passenger car traffic was up 74 percent and bus travel down 11 percent.[16] Among the 33 largest metro-

15. U.S. Department of Commerce, *Survey of Current Business,* vol. 54 (July 1974), p. 24.
16. U.S. Department of Transportation, "1972 National Transportation Report" (DOT, 1972; processed), p. 2-137.

politan areas with over a million population, a dozen experienced 60 to 100 percent gains in auto commuting, while transit rides in most cases were off 20 percent or more. For the journey to work, auto travel was up 55 percent on the average, which explains the congestion that frustrates the commuter.

Trip data for 1970 show that out of every ten employed persons living in the central city of a metropolitan area, seven went to work by automobile, while only two used public transit. (The other walked, worked at home, or used some other method of travel.) In five large metropolitan areas, 85 to 93 percent of central city residents with jobs were automobile commuters.[17] The suburbs in all cases were dependent on cars: 84 percent of all suburban residents with a job drove to work. Trips for shopping, recreation, and social visits, which represent the major part of urban travel, were even more dependent on the automobile.[18]

The overall picture, however, does not convey the extent to which several large metropolitan areas rely on public transportation for the work trip. They are the older, high-density areas where development took place before the automobile. Among these are New York, where 61 percent of the residents use public transit to go to work; Boston (38 percent); Philadelphia (37 percent); and Chicago (36 percent).[19] Fourteen metropolitan areas account for 70 percent of the nation's transit passengers, and the New York area alone accounts for 38 percent.[20]

According to the last census over 8 million households in metropolitan areas lacked cars in 1970—an increase of 4 percent in ten years. In central cities such as Chicago, Philadelphia, Baltimore, Washington, and Boston, 40 percent or more of all households were dependent on public transportation or on walking. In New York City the figure was 58 percent, up 100,000 since 1960.[21] While the number of cars in the nation continues to increase, many of the additions are second and third cars.

The transit problem that is now the focus of federal attention therefore

17. Anaheim-Garden Grove-Santa Ana, San Jose, and San Bernardino-Riverside-Ontario (all in California); and Tampa-St. Petersburg, Florida, and Houston, Texas.

18. The data in this paragraph are from AIP and MVMA, *Urban Transportation Factbook*, pp. I-22, I-23.

19. Ibid., p. I-55.

20. U.S. Department of Transportation, "Feasibility of Federal Assistance for Urban Mass Transportation Operating Costs" (DOT, 1971; processed), p. 9. The 14 areas include the following central cities and their surrounding metropolitan regions: New York, Chicago, Philadelphia, Boston, San Francisco, Washington, Los Angeles, Detroit, Cincinnati, Pittsburgh, Cleveland, St. Louis, Baltimore, and Minneapolis.

21. Data on household car ownership are from AIP and MVMA, *Urban Transportation Factbook*, p. I-74.

involves several distinct elements. Everywhere there is a need to supply public transportation for those who must depend on it. It is also necessary to improve service in the 14 major transit areas that account for 70 percent of all transit riders. Most of these areas have high population densities and a relatively large number of people without cars, and they seem least able to accommodate more automobiles. But the majority have obsolete transit facilities that provide a poor standard of service. At the other extreme are the nation's 178 smaller metropolitan areas with populations of up to 500,000.[22] They rely heavily on automobiles and will continue to do so, but they also include many residents without cars who need public transit that is not now being provided.

Midway between the 14 major transit areas and the 178 smaller areas are 51 cities with populations of over 500,000 in which public transit carries considerable numbers of people and is experiencing the acute financial difficulties that plague most urban transit systems. In these urban areas the issue is whether to build some type of rail rapid transit on exclusive rights-of-way, and if so what kind. The alternative would be to expand and improve bus service and to implement good traffic management and pricing policies that might promote a shift of traffic from autos to buses. In these cities a higher ratio of public to private transport (and of rapid transit to total transit) is thought to be the best way to strengthen transit finances, alleviate congestion, improve service, satisfy the needs of those without cars, and clean up the environment.

Trends in the Location of People and Jobs

The difficulty of making the shift from automobile to transit has been magnified by what has been happening to the location of people and jobs.[23] While metropolitan area population as a whole increased nearly 17 percent from 1960 to 1970 and that of suburban areas increased 33 percent, a gain of only 0.1 percent was registered by the central cities. The older cities of the Northeast and Midwest, where most transit riders live, have been steadily losing people. Since many of the families that remain have low incomes and are without cars, it cannot be said that the need for public transportation is less; the problem of financing good public transit is greater than ever.

The changing location of workplaces has also affected transit adversely (see

22. See ibid., p. I-8.
23. See ibid. for population and employment data in this section.

Table 1-2. Change in the Location of Jobs, by Region and Selected Metropolitan Areas, 1960-70

	Change in number of workers			
	Central city		Outside central city	
Region or area	Thousands	Percent	Thousands	Percent
Region [a]				
Northeast	−513	−10	738	24
North Central	−464	−11	1,712	79
South	332	14	1,016	100
West	359	12	1,063	51
Metropolitan area				
New York	−307	−10	237	32
Chicago	−229	−15	495	70
Detroit	−156	−22	325	61
Philadelphia	−97	−11	177	28
Miami	1	1	121	83
San Francisco-Oakland	1	b	104	23
Dallas	114	38	72	73

Source: American Institute of Planners and Motor Vehicle Manufacturers Association of the U.S., *Urban Transportation Fact Book* (Detroit: MVMA, 1974), pp. I-16, I-17.
a. Data are for the 33 largest metropolitan areas by region.
b. Negligible.

table 1-2). Eleven of the central cities lost a total of a million jobs between 1960 and 1970.[24] In the 125 metropolitan areas with over 250,000 population, there were 41 million jobs in 1970, but not much more than half of them (23 million) were in central cities. The rest were in the suburbs and frequently in rural areas beyond the metropolis.[25]

These changes in the location of jobs and people have had a major impact on home-to-work travel routes. In metropolitan areas of a million people or more, the number of daily work trips beginning and ending in the central city fell by 1.2 million during the 1960s. Work trips into the central city from surrounding areas increased by nearly a million. Reverse commuting from central cities outward to the suburban ring increased by about the same number. But commuting that began and ended in the suburbs showed the largest gain of all, an increase of 3.6 million trips, most of these trips by automobile.

These changing trip patterns and the extent of their dependence on the

24. New York, Chicago, Detroit, Philadelphia, Cleveland, St. Louis, Buffalo, Boston, Milwaukee, Atlanta, and Newark.
25. Center cities have continued to lose population since 1970, and the suburbs and smaller cities have continued to register gains. The nation's economic and social problems, plus factors that are often difficult to identify, have also caused a sharp decline in center city jobs.

Table 1-3. Change in the Method of Getting to Work, Selected Metropolitan Areas, 1960-70

Percent

Metropolitan area[a]	Change in number of work trips via automobile	Change in number of work trips via public transit
Houston	97	−15
Washington, D.C.[b]	84	4
Atlanta	82	−20
Dallas	73	−15
Cincinnati[b]	66	−37
Denver	61	−37
San Diego	56	−65
New Orleans	64	−20
Tampa-St. Petersburg	64	−39
Seattle-Everett	50	−19
Miami	70	2
Baltimore	54	−11
Kansas City[b]	54	−43
Minneapolis-St. Paul	52	−16
Portland[b]	48	−25
St. Louis[b]	45	−45
Milwaukee	52	−33
Cleveland	42	−28
Philadelphia[b]	41	−12
Detroit	34	−26
Chicago	46	−13
San Francisco-Oakland	33	1
Los Angeles-Long Beach	32	−21
Boston	34	−9
New York	46	−4
Pittsburgh	26	−20
Buffalo	25	−33

Source: American Institute of Planners and Motor Vehicle Manufacturers Association of the U.S., *Urban Transportation Fact Book* (Detroit: MVMA, 1974), p. I-23.

a. Selected metropolitan areas of 1 million or more population.

b. Includes the areas in adjacent states that are socially and economically integrated with the central city.

automobile (table 1-3) have raised obvious questions for federal policymakers. The old radial form of rapid transit, from suburb to central city, is no longer an answer to many of the public transit needs of cities and suburbs, and serving low-density suburban areas is a task ill-suited to a fixed-route service by bus. To date, experimentation with the use of demand-responsive transit systems such as dial-a-bus have proved to be too costly, and for many urban trips there is no satisfactory transit substitute for the automobile.

2

Federal Aid and Key Policy Issues

For many years federal transportation policy ignored the problems of the cities. In fact, federal highway aid at one time could not be applied in places with a population of 2,500 or more. The major problem then was to build all-weather rural roads, and the agency in charge of road building at the federal level was the U.S. Department of Agriculture. But with the reorganization and revision of road policy that took place in the 1930s and 1940s, federal aid was transferred from the Agriculture Department and expanded to include an urban road program that would eventually create thousands of miles of urban expressways and an extensive system of federal aid for city streets.

Defects in the federal approach to urban transportation were, first, that it ignored public transit and, second, that it paid little if any attention to the interrelationship between transportation and the other aspects of urban development. By the early 1960s the first of these omissions was corrected by the initiation of a continuing transit aid program that has now become a multi-billion-dollar effort. This policy reversal has been accompanied by a substantial liberalization of federal aid for highways that is moving rapidly in the direction of a unified transportation program for urban areas. The second defect may be overcome by a transportation planning process that relates the financing of transportation facilities and services to comprehensive programs for the long-term development and redevelopment of urbanized areas.

An Overview of Federal Programs

A continuing program of federal aid for urban transportation began in 1944, when urban highways were made part of the established program of federal aid for state highways. But the highways eligible for aid were the extensions of rural highways through and around cities and were never con-

14

sidered an integral part of the urban transportation system. The objective was rather to facilitate intercity movement by the removal of urban obstacles.

Today the emphasis continues to be on intercity routes through and around urban areas as the Interstate Highway System has become the major focus of the federal highway program. A total of 8,800 miles of urban highways are included in the 42,500-mile interstate network, which is now 85 percent completed with a current price tag of more than $70 billion. The federal share of the total cost has been 90 percent. In addition to the interstate mileage, work continues to be done on the 39,000 miles of urban extensions of state primary and secondary highways that are eligible for federal aid, and an additional urban system was recently authorized that includes other major streets not in the primary or secondary systems. This new network is expected to total as many as 190,000 miles.[1]

Federal aid for urban public transit did not begin until after the passage of the Urban Mass Transportation Assistance Act of 1964, which established the first major program of capital grant assistance for mass transportation, following a transit demonstration program and a program of low-interest loans for transit facilities that began in 1961.[2] In 1970 Congress stated its intent to make $10 billion available for transit investments over a 12-year period and authorized the expenditure of an initial $3.1 billion. The total transit authorization was later doubled.[3] The federal government paid two-thirds of the costs of transit equipment and other capital investments (but 90 percent for interstate highways) until 1973 when this proportion was increased to 80 percent.

The actual amount of aid for transit was relatively modest through 1970, amounting to about 4 percent of total federal outlays for urban transportation during the 1960s. For fiscal 1975, however, the program authorization had been increased to $1.4 billion, ten times the 1970 level.[4]

From these increased funds, about $3 billion of federal aid had been made

1. Data on the interstate and urban highway systems are from Motor Vehicle Manufacturers Association of the U.S., *1973/74 Automobile Facts and Figures* (Detroit: MVMA, n.d.), p. 46; MVMA, *1975 Automobile Facts and Figures* (Detroit: MVMA, n.d.), p. 49; and Highway Users Federation, *Highways, Safety and Transit: An Analysis of the Federal-Aid Highway Act of 1973* (Washington, D.C.: HUF, 1973), p. 5.

2. See George W. Hilton, *Federal Transit Subsidies: The Urban Mass Transportation Assistance Program* (American Enterprise Institute for Public Policy Research, 1974), pp. 5-11, for a history of the early legislation.

3. These authorizations were the result of the Urban Mass Transportation Assistance Act of 1970 and the Federal-Aid Highway Act of 1973.

4. *The Budget of the United States Government—Appendix, Fiscal Year 1975*, p. 713.

available by mid-1974 under the Urban Mass Transportation Administration (UMTA) for 750 different capital grant projects. The program had helped 230 cities purchase 20,000 buses, and bus acquisitions accounted for one-third of the funds expended. A small group of six cities with rapid transit had been helped to construct 200 miles of new rail rapid transit lines and to buy new rail cars, and these grants accounted for 60 percent of all federal transit aid. Other funds were used to help public agencies purchase private transit companies, and 90 cities were included in this program.[5]

The nature of the UMTA program is illustrated by the 75 grants made during the month of June 1974, involving a total of $267 million. The grants ranged from $12,000 to Virginia Polytechnic Institute to develop a methodology for evaluating transit system compliance with civil rights requirements to $50 million in supplemental grants to help pay for Atlanta's rapid transit. In general these allocations consisted of a large number of small grants for transit planning, often insignificant in amount; a small number of large grants for rail transport; and a considerable number of moderate-sized grants for bus purchases and for the takeover of private transit companies. But the major funding was for rail rapid transit, including new systems.[6]

These federal grants were in addition to state and local sources of transit financing: 17 states and over 80 cities have taken steps of their own to aid mass transportation systems. As early as 1967 New York provided $1 billion for transit capital grants from a transportation bond issue, and both Pennsylvania and New Jersey provided transit operating subsidies. Massachusetts began paying 90 percent of the debt service on transit bonds for the Massachusetts Bay Transportation Authority from a state cigarette tax. Other states initiated various forms of tax exemptions, rebates, and reimbursements for fare discounts, while many local governments provided annual operating assistance to compensate for deficits.[7] In 1972 state and local governments were contributing half again as much aid as the federal government.[8]

5. "Mass Transit: Progress and Problems," Remarks by Secretary of Transportation Claude S. Brinegar at Meeting of Society of Automotive Engineers, Anaheim, Calif., August 14, 1974, *Department of Transportation News*, 05-S-74, p. 5. UMTA was established in 1968 to administer the federal urban mass transportation program.

6. U.S. Department of Transportation, "A Study of Urban Mass Transportation Needs and Financing" (Government Printing Office, 1974; processed), p. IV-16.

7. For information about state and local transit financing, see U.S. Department of Transportation, "Feasibility of Federal Assistance for Urban Mass Transportation Operating Costs" (DOT, 1971; processed), chap. 3.

8. Department of Transportation, "A Study of Urban Mass Transportation Needs," p. IV-16.

Recent Federal Aid Revisions

National legislation in recent years has altered the federal approach to urban transportation still further. Highway legislation in 1973 made possible for the first time the use of road money for urban mass transit. Transit aid in 1974 put transit financing on a long-term basis, with part of the money to be distributed among urbanized areas by formula. It also made federal money available for operating subsidies as well as capital investment.

The Federal-Aid Highway Act of 1973 authorized nearly $18 billion for highways over the three-year period 1973-76. Most of the money ($16.7 billion) has come from the Highway Trust Fund, the repository of federal motor vehicle and petroleum excise taxes that have been earmarked for highways. An estimated $2.6 billion of this will be spent for urban highways.[9] Matching provisions call for 70 percent federal financing of noninterstate highway programs—a change from the previous 50-50 matching provisions that became effective in 1974.

The move toward a unified urban transportation program was strengthened by two financial provisions in the 1973 highway legislation. Highway funds allocated to the urban system can now be used for transit projects instead of roads at the option of the local government. Additional provisions make it possible for cities to forgo the construction of further urban interstate highway links and instead to obtain an equivalent amount of general funds from the federal government to pay for alternative transit. There has been only limited use of these provisions, but examples include the use of funds previously reserved for highways for bus and rail projects under the New York City Transit Authority and the approval granted to the Massachusetts Bay Transportation Authority in Boston to withdraw $600 million from interstate funds for transit.[10]

Other aspects of the highway program extend the scope of permissible expenditures far beyond the construction of new roads to programs for improved highway operations and safety, the acquisition of highway rights-of-way for transit, the construction of special lanes for buses, preferential treatment of transit through traffic controls, and the financing of parking space at

9. This figure is derived from past experience indicating that half the $3 billion authorized for the Interstate Highway System by the Federal-Aid Highway Act of 1973 will be spent on urban sections. The balance includes $300 million provided in the act for extensions of state highways within cities, $800 million for the urban system, and $50 million for special highways connecting the interstate system in urbanized areas.

10. *Department of Transportation News,* UMTA, 119-74, July 9, 1974; and information provided by the Department of Transportation.

transit stops. The creation of exclusive bus lanes and busways to expedite bus movement can also be financed through the highway program. But as yet there are only isolated cases of this use of road funds, and no community-wide efforts have been made to combine the two programs.

The National Mass Transportation Assistance Act of 1974 authorized the expenditure of $11.854 billion for the period 1975 through 1980: $11.3 billion for urban mass transportation and $500 million for rural mass transit. The $11.3 billion of urban money is divided two ways. The distribution of $3.975 billion among cities of 50,000 population or more is to be used for either capital investments or to pay transit operating subsidies. Federal-local matching provisions are up to 80-20 for construction projects and up to 50-50 if grants are used for operating costs. The other $7.325 billion made available by the transit program is allocated to capital projects subject to approval by the secretary of transportation. The act provides for federal matching of up to 80 percent of the cost of these capital projects.

The distribution of the nearly $4 billion of either capital or operating assistance is based on a formula that gives equal weight to urban population size and to population density. These formula funds were made available at the rate of $300 million in fiscal 1975, and the amount will increase each year thereafter to a level of $900 million by 1980.

Under the formula distribution, $1 billion of the $4 billion total goes to two urban areas—New York and Los Angeles. The New York-New Jersey area will receive $707 million, or an average of $118 million annually, while the second largest allotment, to Los Angeles, will total $318 million, or $53 million a year. Boston gets $14 million annually, Baltimore $10 million, and Houston $8 million. (See table 2-1.) The difficulty of reflecting needs in a formula distribution based on population can be seen in the fact that Los Angeles, with only 153 million annual trips by transit, gets nearly half as much money as the New York area where there are 12 times as many transit riders and 45 percent of all households lack cars. San Diego, with 13 million transit riders a year, gets the same allotment as Milwaukee, with 63 million.[11] No formula could be found that proved wholly satisfactory.

In the case of both formula grants and capital assistance for specific projects, the new legislation requires the recipients of aid to submit a total urban transportation plan as a condition for participating in the program. These

11. Household car ownership and transit data are from American Institute of Planners and Motor Vehicle Manufacturers Association of the U.S., *Urban Transportation Factbook* (Detroit: MVMA, 1974), pp. I-25, I-29.

Table 2-1. Projected Apportionment of Federal Transit Aid Funds, Selected Urbanized Areas, 1975-80[a]

Millions of dollars

	Transit aid	
Urbanized area	Total, 1975-80	Annual average
New York-New Jersey	707	118
Los Angeles-Long Beach	318	53
Chicago	253	42
Philadelphia	153	25
Detroit	139	23
San Francisco-Oakland	102	17
Boston	87	14
Washington	91	15
Cleveland	56	9
St. Louis	62	10
Pittsburgh	53	9
Minneapolis-St. Paul	44	7
Houston	49	8
Baltimore	59	10
Dallas	33	5
Milwaukee	34	6
Seattle-Everett	35	6
Miami	43	7
San Diego	35	6
Atlanta	32	5

Source: *Federal Register,* vol. 40 (January 13, 1975), pt. 1, p. 2540.
a. Funds authorized under the National Mass Transportation Assistance Act of 1974.

plans must conform with overall urban development plans and include measures to improve the efficiency of transport operations and to conserve energy, improve air quality, and increase social and environmental amenity. Such measures may include the revision of transit fare policies, preferential treatment of transit through traffic regulations, the introduction of staggered work hours, the designation of all-bus lanes, and the encouragement of car pools. Beginning in March 1977 the annual program of an area's projects will not be approved unless supported by evidence that reasonable progress has been made in implementing previously programmed projects. UMTA will strengthen the process of determining appropriate capital investments by requiring cities to analyze the costs and benefits of alternative projects.[12]

12. *Federal Register,* vol. 40 (August 1, 1975), pt. 3, pp. 32546-47; and ibid. (September 17, 1975), pt. 2, pp. 42976-84.

Basic Unresolved Issues

The "1974 National Transportation Report," a cooperative study by state and local governments that deals with transit and highway needs between 1972 and 1990, indicates the magnitude of projected capital expenditures for urban transportation.[13] In 241 urbanized areas during this period the proposed outlays total one-quarter of a trillion dollars. Whatever the exact amount, these expenditures will have a powerful influence on the future of the cities, and the future of the cities is not being thought about very much as urban areas vie for a share in the 80 percent federal inducement to invest in new capital projects for public transit.

Two-thirds of the $62 billion of capital outlays now planned for transit is for rail systems, a proportion that suggests the importance to the cities of the decisions now being made for transportation. Bus systems, which are expected to account for 68 percent of the nationwide increase in transit ridership, would involve only 13 percent of the capital cost.[14] And although the $62 billion spent for transit may double the number of transit passengers by 1990, according to Department of Transportation estimates this increase would mean that the level of transit patronage would be no higher than it was in 1950.[15] The resulting annual net operating deficits are expected to increase from close to $1 billion in 1972 to $2.5 billion by 1990, but this seems to be an unrealistically conservative estimate.[16]

The figures are disconcerting, and they pose some urgent questions.

—Is it desirable to use 67 percent of available capital for rail systems that will accommodate only a very small percentage of riders? What should be the federal position on rail rapid transit versus buses? Should the federal government be tempting the cities to adopt highly capital-intensive solutions in the face of so many other needs?

13. U.S. Department of Transportation, "1974 National Transportation Report" (Government Printing Office, 1974; processed). Cost data in this section are in 1971 constant dollars.

14. Ibid., p. V-8.

15. Department of Transportation, "A Study of Urban Mass Transportation Needs," p. 1-4; and American Public Transit Association, *'74-'75 Transit Fact Book* (Washington, D.C.: APTA, 1975), p. 14.

16. Department of Transportation, ibid., pp. III-30. Actually, transit deficits for as early as 1981 have been estimated at $4 billion. See "Remarks by Robert E. Patricelli, Administrator, Urban Mass Transportation Administration, before the Fifth Annual Legislative Conference on Transportation, New York, N.Y., October 21, 1975," *Department of Transportation News* (DOT, n.d.), p. 3.

—Since the proportion of urban trips by transit is not expected to change, even after the expenditure of $62 billion in new capital, what are the alternatives? Could more effective results be achieved through efforts to increase the operating efficiency of the urban transport system as a whole? Could buses and taxis, combined with tax and pricing policies, regulations, and other low-cost solutions bring about a greater shift from automobile to public transportation?

—If the efforts of public agencies to expand public transit are to have the very limited results now anticipated, there is urgent need to assure the continuation of essential automobile services. But how is this to be reconciled with the outlook for energy supplies and prices?

—In view of the long-term outlook for energy, is federal policy focusing sufficiently on the research and development necessary to accelerate the discovery of alternative transport technologies? And how can urban growth policies and community design be made consistent with efforts to solve the transportation problem?

Transportation investment alone has not helped very much to resolve the problems of urban congestion anywhere in the world. There is strong evidence that the characteristics of the cities themselves are the reason for the persistence of transport problems and that only an attack on urban design, environmental deterioration, and the plight of the urban population itself can help make cities and their transportation more manageable. There is a danger that an overcommitment to transport investment—and particularly to rail rapid transit—may leave the cities less capable than ever of solving their basic problems.

3

The Large Investment Option: Rapid Transit

The subway, or metro, is being viewed in many cities as the most effective remedy for urban congestion, and the public responds far more enthusiastically to the prospect of a new subway than to measures for increasing the efficiency of existing means of transportation. Thus far, however, big cities in the United States have not relied heavily on rail rapid transit with the exception of New York, which has 237 route miles and accounts for 80 percent of all rapid transit riders in the country.[1] Only four other U.S. cities have long-established subway and rapid transit systems—90 miles in Chicago, 64 in Boston, 32 in Cleveland, and 29 in Philadelphia. (See table 3-1.) But the situation is changing, with San Francisco's new Bay Area Rapid Transit (BART) system in operation, rapid transit under way in Washington and Atlanta, and the ground broken for a subway in Baltimore. Other cities have done substantial planning for such systems, including Denver, Pittsburgh, and Los Angeles. Federal aid has been a major factor in the trend, but there is still no clear consensus about whether the benefits warrant the costs.

As mentioned in chapter 2, 60 percent of the federal money thus far made available to the cities for public transit has been used for rail systems, and projections of need suggest even greater emphasis on rail facilities over the next decade and a half. In the nation's nine largest cities, rail transit is expected to absorb 90 percent of federal transit aid in the future.[2] Some of the allocation to rail facilities will be used to upgrade equipment and operations on existing rapid transit facilities, but most of it is expected to go into new sys-

1. American Institute of Planners and Motor Vehicle Manufacturers Association of the U.S., *Urban Transportation Factbook* (Detroit: MVMA, 1974), p. I-29.
2. The nine cities are New York, Chicago, Los Angeles, Boston, Philadelphia, Cleveland, Detroit, San Francisco, and Washington. New York alone would absorb $16 billion. (U.S. Department of Transportation, "A Study of Urban Mass Transportation Needs and Financing" [Government Printing Office, 1974; processed], p. I-3.)

Table 3-1. Characteristics of North American Cities That Have Rail Rapid
Transit Systems

City	Population, 1970[a] (millions)		Population per square mile, central city, 1970[a] (thousands)	Employment in central city, 1970[b] (thousands)	Rail rapid transit route miles, 1975
	Urbanized area	Central city			
New York	11.6	7.9	24.4	2,885	237
Chicago	7.0	3.3	12.3	1,349	90
Philadelphia	4.8	1.9	15.2	772	29
Boston	2.8	0.6	13.9	374	64
Cleveland	2.1	0.7	9.9	392	32
Toronto	2.6	0.7	17.8	n.a.	21
Montreal	2.7	1.2	20.9	n.a.	16
San Francisco	3.1	1.1	10.0	556	71
Washington[c]	2.9	0.8	12.3	492	98
Atlanta[c]	1.4	0.5	3.8	288	50[d]

Sources: American Institute of Planners and Motor Vehicle Manufacturers Association
of the U.S., *Urban Transportation Factbook* (Detroit: MVMA, 1974), pp. I-9, I-10, I-42-
44, I-82; John Paxton, ed., *The Statesman's Year-Book, 1973-1974* (St. Martins Press,
1973), p. 240; *Encyclopaedia Britannica* (1973), vols. 15 and 22, pp. 798, 90, respec-
tively; and information provided by the individual transit systems.

n.a. Not available.
a. 1971 for Toronto and Montreal.
b. Number of residents in the urbanized area that are working in the central city.
c. Subway under construction.
d. The rapid transit system will have an additional 14 miles of exclusive busways.

tems. The magnitude of the expenditures now being contemplated stresses
the need for a careful analysis of costs and benefits and of possible alternative
solutions.

In other parts of the world large cities such as Tokyo, London, and Paris
rely heavily on rail systems. The past decade has seen new subways built in
Rotterdam, Madrid, Munich, Milan, Paris, and other European cities, as well
as in Toronto, Montreal, and Mexico City. Subway construction is under way
in São Paulo and Rio de Janeiro, and studies of possible new metros have
recently been made in Singapore, Hong Kong, Caracas, and Teheran.

Criteria for Rapid Transit

Cities with rapid transit all have large populations and high population densities. New York has 24,000 people per square mile, which makes it by far the
most densely populated city in the United States. Boston, with 14,000 people
per square mile, and Philadelphia, with more than 15,000, are also well above
the suggested minimum of 10,000 people per square mile for economically

feasible rapid transit in U.S. urban areas. For conditions to be fully favorable to rapid transit, a population of 2 million is suggested and a density of 14,000 people per square mile.[3]

Montreal and Toronto both have densities approaching that of New York. In Toronto a 21-mile automated subway is carrying over 100 million passengers annually—one-third of the city's public transit riders and about the same number that the Boston and Chicago subways each carry. An additional 64 million people in Toronto are riding streetcars each year; thus rail carries more than half of all the city's public transit riders. In Montreal 16 miles of subway with pneumatic-tired trains running on a concrete track carry 63 million passengers a year, almost one-third of total transit passengers.

In addition to population criteria, factors governing the rapid transit decision include the physical shape of the urban area (a linear city is better adapted to rapid transit than a circular area requiring many routes), topography and natural obstacles, and the proportion of the route mileage that could be built on the surface rather than in costly underground tubes. Surface costs can also be reduced if rights-of-way are already available along freeways or railroads. Where capital costs are as much as 15 to 20 cents per passenger mile, or more than operating a car, rapid transit may be a mistake.[4]

Although few U.S. cities other than those that are now operating or building rail rapid transit systems could qualify for such systems on the basis of population, population density, and central city employment, eight cities had rapid transit plans under consideration at the end of 1975. But as Atlanta demonstrates, cities that do not need rapid transit at present may nevertheless opt for it as a means of influencing future development toward higher densities. Yet a dense central city is not necessarily a prerequisite for rapid transit. The criterion for building subways may be corridor travel volumes rather than the population density at the center, as in systems like BART and the Washington Metro that extend well beyond central cities into suburbia.

Federal aid is being used for new rail rapid transit systems in several major metropolitan areas. The Washington Metro, partially financed by a special federal grant of more than $1 billion, will be an automated system of 98 miles, 47 in subway, connecting the District of Columbia and outlying points in Maryland and Virginia. A section of this most costly system (at least $5 bil-

3. Wilbur Smith and Associates, "Urban Transportation Concepts: Center City Transportation Project," prepared for the U.S. Department of Transportation (Smith and Associates, 1970; processed), p. 95.

4. Thomas B. Deen, "Critical Decisions in the Rapid Transit Planning Process" (paper presented at the Georgia State University Seminar, Atlanta, August 5, 1974; processed).

lion) will be opened in 1976, and completion of the total system is scheduled for 1981. The Metropolitan Atlanta Rapid Transit Authority (MARTA) has begun construction of a 64-mile combined rail-bus rapid transit system, with 50 miles of rail facilities, 9 underground, 16 on aerial structures, and 25 at grade. Fourteen miles of highway lanes for buses only will complete the system. The Urban Mass Transit Administration (UMTA) has obligated $500 million for the first 8.5 miles of Baltimore's planned 50-mile system, and Pittsburgh is also scheduled to obtain federal support for rapid transit.[5]

Experience with San Francisco's BART

The first information about how these systems may perform is being provided by San Francisco's automated 71-mile BART system (with 20 miles in subway).[6] BART provides an excellent high-speed ride (80-mile-per-hour maximum) in quiet air-conditioned cars that serve attractive stations along commuter routes that converge on San Francisco from Berkeley, Oakland, and other points. Federal aid for this system has totaled $312 million, or about 20 percent of the estimated total capital cost of more than $1.6 billion.

Although BART achieved system-wide operation in September 1974, it did so on a limited five-day week and without evening service due to lack of cars, the high rate of car breakdowns, and the lengthy headways required for safety pending improvement in the reliability of the electronic controls. Thus the rate of 125,000 passengers carried daily during October 1975 was substantially below the full-service patronage projected for BART when the system was being planned (200,000 passengers a day and 60 million rides a year).

The BART system is being evaluated in a comprehensive study financed by the Department of Transportation and the Department of Housing and Urban Development. This BART Impact Program will analyze the effect of rapid transit on travel practices, highway congestion, land use, public finance, and the environment. Cities contemplating new rapid transit systems should be able to benefit from the results of these investigations, some of which are even now yielding useful data.

Preliminary findings provide some indication of the possible impact BART may have when full operations are under way. Financially, the picture is not

5. Data are from releases prepared by the offices of the various rapid transit systems and from newspaper reports.
6. Data on BART are from the Metropolitan Transportation Commission, Berkeley, California.

encouraging. With a projected level of 31 million passengers in fiscal year 1976, the average subsidy per ride will be about $2.50, including $1.40 in debt service and $1.08 in operating subsidy. A passenger from downtown San Francisco to Berkeley pays 85 cents according to the present fare structure, but the cost of providing the trip will be $3.30. Disregarding capital costs, which are to be paid from nonuser sources, BART fares in fiscal 1976 are expected to cover less than half the operating costs.

BART is primarily a home-to-work commuter system, with about 70 percent of the riders using the system for this purpose. The second most frequent use is to get to school or college, which accounts for 10 to 15 percent of the travel. The average trip length after the bay tube opened was estimated to be 14 miles, which reflects the long-distance city-to-suburb nature of BART travel.

The commuter railway system provided by BART is quite different from a system designed to provide circulation within a central city, and this difference is seen in comparative data for Toronto. BART's route mileage is more than triple that of Toronto's, yet even if traffic on BART rises to the projected level of 60 million in 1976–77, this will still be only about one-fifth the number of passengers using the Toronto metro. The Toronto system is designed with short distances between stations to accommodate local trips within the city and thus carries many passengers on short journeys. BART was not intended to be used for short trips, either to work or for local shopping, and its routes and stops are inconvenient for this type of travel.

BART's effect on land use and the environment is not yet fully known. In some locations (Berkeley and San Francisco, for example) the station areas and subway construction routes have provided an opportunity for substantial remodeling of the streets. There have also been successful efforts to introduce landscaping along BART elevated structures. Many of these structures parallel freeways or railways and therefore have added only marginally to negative environmental factors. But in other cases the noise and neighborhood barriers introduced by the surface and elevated routes are definitely a negative aspect.

BART's influence on dispersal could be important. Although it is too early to tell, it is doubtful that BART will have the centralizing effects that planners initially expected it to have. Indeed the opposite is always a possibility. The net out-migration of families who can move to suburbia and take advantage of the subsidized commuter fares could make a major change in the character of the city, and economic activity could also shift to city centers outside San Francisco that have been made more accessible by the rapid transit service.

On the other hand, BART may not have any of the major effects once considered likely, because a relatively small number of total daily trips will be taken on the system. To illustrate, in 1970, before BART, there were 1,014,000 workers in the three-county BART district. Of this number 715,000 drove to work (76 percent) and 185,000 used bus or rail facilities (18 percent). When BART eventually carries 100,000 daily round-trip riders, about 70,000 of them will be traveling to and from work, and an estimated 27,000 of these will be former auto travelers. This number is 3.8 percent of the total work trips made by automobile in the three-county area; hence BART's role in reducing auto trips to work will not be substantial.

With respect to all home-to-work traffic by all methods, BART riding will constitute about 8 percent of the area-wide total. But BART will be used for a much smaller percentage of trips for shopping, recreation, and other non-work purposes, which account for two-thirds of all travel in the area. The net effect will probably be that BART will absorb only 2 to 3 percent of total daily trips.

On the important trans-bay route, however, BART's effect may be more significant. In October 1974 daily one-way trips across San Francisco Bay totaled 135,000. Trips by auto totaled 92,400, bus 17,000, and BART 26,100. Thus BART was moving 19 percent of the total traffic crossing the bay. Of those who traveled on BART, 38 percent had previously used the bus and 35 percent had been auto users. Most of the others had not made the trip before. The 9,200 one-way trips taken on BART's trans-bay service by those who were previously auto riders involved about 6,000 cars (at 1.5 persons per car). This number of cars represents about 7 percent of the pre-BART level of automobile traffic on the Bay Bridge, but most of the vacated space has been absorbed by a new influx of motorists.

Together, these findings suggest that low-cost measures to improve the performance of the bus system might have provided benefits equal to or greater than those of the rail rapid transit system. It might also have been more beneficial to build the rail system within the city of San Francisco to improve local circulation, limiting the long-haul system to a trans-bay shuttle service to link Oakland with San Francisco. It has been pointed out as well that the $1.6 billion invested in BART could have provided $16,000 apiece for 100,000 Bay Area families to help finance housing construction, rehabilitation, and neighborhood improvement. Although such a reordering of priorities may be less compelling for the relatively affluent Bay Area, weighing the options seems to be an urgent need in Baltimore, St. Louis, and other older cities.

Advantages and Disadvantages of Rapid Transit

Whether or not new rail rapid transit systems offer acceptable solutions for American cities is an unresolved question. On the positive side the speed, comfort, and safety of new subway facilities are impressive, and they permit greater efficiency of movement for considerable numbers of people under high-density conditions. Rapid transit saves space and supplies a fixed physical framework for the development of the urban area. When a fixed facility for transport is constructed, buildings and other structures are likely to follow, and the city becomes more compact, with high-density development centering around the subway stations. This may be desirable or undesirable, depending on how these developments take place and how well they are planned, but the potentials are impressive.

On the negative side, the initial costs of rapid transit are high, substantial operating deficits appear to be inevitable for most cities, capacity is often unnecessarily high, and the inflexible nature of the investment leads to fear of early obsolescence. The rapid transit system may be able to play only a limited role in total urban trip patterns, and those who lack cars and need public transit often cannot make good use of rapid transit.

Obviously rapid transit has a specific function and cannot meet every need. Just as the automobile is inadequate for dense urban corridor travel, so rail rapid transit often is ill-suited for short journeys and crosstown trips. The supply of good transportation in urban areas calls for a mix of different services, both public and private. The question is where and under what circumstances a commitment to rail facilities is warranted.

Because of the high cost of rail rapid transit, the Department of Transportation has attempted to develop substitute bus rapid transit, using busways on expressways for the exclusive use of transit vehicles. The most notable example is the Shirley Highway express bus lane in the median strip of Interstate 95 entering Washington, D.C., from Virginia. The project has expanded bus ridership and increased the speed of transit travel, but again at substantial cost.[7] Other experiments of this type are being conducted in California, New Jersey, and elsewhere. An alternative possibility being considered by the Department of Transportation is light rail transit, an electric streetcar that

7. See U.S. Department of Transportation, *Preferential Treatment for High-Occupancy Vehicles* (DOT, 1974), pp. 3-5. The Shirley Highway has an 11-mile busway in the median strip that saves 10 to 15 minutes a trip for 16,000 round-trip passengers. UMTA funds were used to buy the buses, and interstate highway funds were used to construct the special busway lanes.

uses underground track in heavy-traffic areas of the center city but operates perhaps 70 to 80 percent on the surface, using available rights-of-way such as abandoned railroad tracks or the median strip on expressways. Light rail transit has been developed successfully in several European cities (Brussels, Vienna, Frankfurt) and is much less costly than conventional subways.

Is it worth it, then, to commit large sums to networks like the Washington Metro or San Francisco's BART? Getting traffic underground on heavily traveled routes does make it possible to reduce noise, air pollution, and space requirements for alternative roads and parking. Moreover, the rapid transit investment may not lack economic justification when viewed in relation to the cost of operating the whole urban living system that rapid transit makes possible. It is necessary to extend the analysis beyond transportation to the urban system as a whole, and to assess the total costs and benefits of the entire urban community, with and without rapid transit.

If rapid transit makes possible large cost reductions through high-density land uses and substantial benefits in the organization of economic activity, then the system may be warranted. In other words, it may not be the high cost of rail transportation relative to other transport solutions that is critical, but rather a comparison of the total costs and benefits of alternative urban settlements that can be supported by various transportation solutions.

If rapid transit is to provide effective solutions, however, the effect on urban development cannot be left to chance. Measures must be taken to control location decisions that are made in response to the supply of additional transport capacity. Unless land-use plans conform to transport solutions, excessive high-rise office construction downtown and rising rents are apt to push the residential use of land farther out from the center city. In that case, the new transport capacity must accommodate a fresh crop of commuters, and congestion reappears at a higher level. The management of urban growth must be consistent with transportation policy if rapid transit is to avoid being underutilized or inundated by new traffic generators.

The concern that rapid transit may be underutilized is not without basis as dispersal and resistance to higher densities continues. High-capacity rail lines may be increasingly ill-suited to the low-density patterns and changing life-styles of the typical metropolis. There is no longer the same focus on a single center, but a tendency to disperse concentrations among many centers. The fact is that the future of the American city is uncertain and changing, and the city is a risky setting for expensive and irreversible transport investments.

From an energy-efficiency standpoint, rail rapid transit has further unfavorable aspects. If the need is to expand public transit quickly and to do so for all the nation's cities, a concentration of federal aid on a few rapid transit lines will defeat the purpose. Even if all the $8 billion capital assistance fund provided by the National Mass Transportation Assistance Act of 1974 were to be used for new rail systems, the money would supply no more than five cities with systems equivalent to BART, and total ridership at the end of 10 or 15 years would probably not exceed a million a day. The same amount spent for buses would supply transportation for far more people at the end of the first year and in ten years could supply bus service for as many as 64 million people a day throughout the country.[8]

The reason money spent for buses goes further than money spent for rail rapid transit is that the roadways for buses are already in place, and additional money spent for transit all goes into equipment. Rail rapid transit, however, generally involves new rights-of-way and tunneling that may cost as much as $100 million per mile; thus only a limited amount of service can be delivered for a given sum of money. The economic advantage of the bus derives from its ability to use the multibillion dollar investment in streets. In addition, the bus requires much less initial investment than a rail car, and because of its shorter life it is able to benefit from continuing innovations in technology. But the sharing of the streets with other traffic is often a major drawback, and successful bus operations in heavy traffic will be dependent on whether exclusive lanes or whole rights-of-way can be made available.

In the final analysis, the rapid transit decision should be based not only on an appraisal of transport alternatives but on the financial capacity of the community, the priorities assigned to various public needs, the kind of city the residents would like to have, and the anticipated conditions of growth and change that will dictate transportation requirements. The fact that the federal government pays so much of the cost of rapid transit leads city policymakers to discount these considerations.

8. This example is based on the assumption that there would be $8 billion of federal funds with 20 percent local matching to purchase 160,000 buses at $60,000 each, carrying 400 passengers per bus per workday.

4

The Low-Cost Option: Better Use of Existing Systems

The massive capital investments planned for urban rail rapid transit and doubts about how much they will contribute to the solution of urban problems suggest the need for considering an alternative federal approach. The wiser course might be to make more effective use of the motorized transportation system already available, with emphasis on greater energy efficiency, air pollution control, and the alleviation of municipal budgetary problems. This might prove more satisfactory than attempts to achieve a shift from road to rail and would certainly be much less costly.

The potentials for this option are indicated by the substantial transportation facilities already available. There are 600,000 miles of streets in urban areas, 70 million passenger cars, 170,000 taxis, and 50,000 buses.[1] The more efficient use of these facilities might be achieved by a combination of improved bus and taxi systems, better traffic management, and control of demand through such measures as automobile taxing policies, reduced transit fares, increased parking fees, and the staggering of work hours. Current legislation empowers the federal government to promote such efficiency measures as a condition for the receipt of federal aid.

Guideline for Grants

The difficulties of carrying out a conditional grant program to remedy transportation problems are well known. What appear to be sensible measures to increase efficiency, such as the elimination of curbside parking, the creation

1. Motor Vehicle Manufacturers Association of the U.S., *1973/74 Automobile Facts and Figures* (Detroit: MVMA, n.d.), p. 46; and John D. Wells and others, *Economic Characteristics of the Urban Public Transportation Industry,* prepared for the U.S. Department of Transportation (Government Printing Office, 1972), p. 2-2. Number of cars is author's estimate.

of pedestrian malls, or the staggering of work hours are prescriptions that have aroused sharp debate and generally successful resistance. But local governments prevented from taking these steps by pressures from motorists, merchants, and property owners might welcome the imposition of federal requirements as a means of strengthening the hand of municipal authorities—even at this stage of the new federalism.

There are signs around the world that suggest a declining resistance to innovations in urban traffic management. Merchants in Stockholm, Cologne, The Hague, and other European cities have come to appreciate the all-pedestrian streets they fought against for so many years. Swedish motorists have endorsed car-free zones in central business districts, and cities such as Hamburg, Göteborg, and Vienna have introduced a variety of schemes for restricting automobile use and for giving preference to public transit.[2] In the United States there are moves in the same direction, with emphasis on designating special bus lanes, increasing downtown parking rates, eliminating parking on the street, and restricting truck transport in rush hours.

These trends will be reinforced to an important degree by efforts to comply with the clear air legislation of 1970, which imposed limits on the amounts of air pollution that will be permitted. Pollutants associated with transportation will ultimately be resolved by vehicle design, but the immediate task of meeting minimum requirements by 1977 is forcing the adoption of strategies for limiting motor vehicle usage. Thus in California a series of state transportation control plans are being developed that rely on the expansion of bus transport, the designation of exclusive lanes for buses and car pools, and the management of parking. These plans could reduce statewide travel in 1977 by as much as 12 percent, with maximum effect (a 20 percent reduction) in the Los Angeles area.[3] It is possible that higher fuel prices and other increases in the cost of motoring will contribute to the reduction in total travel.

Federal regulation of state and local transport operations has a number of precedents. In early 1974 the government imposed a nationwide speed limit of 55 miles an hour as a means of conserving fuel. Laxity in state enforcement of the limit led to a proposal in Congress to withdraw federal highway funds from offending states. It was not the first time an effort had been made to exact a price for highway aid. States "diverting" the proceeds of special highway-user taxes to nonhighway purposes have long been subject to reductions in federal highway allocations.[4]

2. See Wilfred Owen, *The Accessible City* (Brookings Institution, 1972), pp. 104-6.
3. Information from California State Department of Transportation.
4. 48 Stat. 995, sec. 12; 23 U.S.C. (1970 ed.) 126.

Other precedents in federal highway law have included the stipulations that to be eligible for federal assistance states must designate a federally approved system of routes and must design new facilities to conform to specified standards. Federally aided roads have to be maintained at acceptable levels of physical quality, and failure to conform may mean the loss of up to two-thirds of future federal support.[5]

Grants for urban highways and for transit are now being made contingent on a general set of conditions that eventually will require every urban area to have a physical transportation plan, an operating strategy for all methods of movement, and, it is hoped, a financial strategy that includes price and tax policies. Ideally, a physical plan should include an integrated network designed to achieve desirable standards for both public and private transportation in ways that minimize unwanted side effects and keep social costs at a minimum. And transportation development should be an integral part of total community development. The physical plan might include transit networks that bring the majority of people within a stipulated distance of a transit stop; networks of bus streets or bus lanes to separate bus operation from cars; and the development of integrated transit, parking, and taxi systems. The operating strategy should include environmental considerations—noise, vibration, and pollution—and service standards. The latter, while differing among cities, might include such factors as schedule frequency and reliability, age of equipment, comfort, speed, and safety. Financial plans should be concerned with the level and structure of transit fares, automobile-user charges, and taxi rates and parking fees, and pricing should be viewed not only as a source of revenue but as an aid to making economic choices among travel options. These goals and criteria could provide useful guidelines for programming future expenditures.

Pricing Transportation Services

Among the principal methods of increasing the effective delivery of transportation services is the revision of pricing policies, which have generally favored the automobile and, at least until recently, have proved disadvantageous to the transit rider. The situation is essentially this: a person driving to work in a central city is likely to be paying insufficient average taxes per mile to cover the extra costs of peak-hour highway capacity, and he may enjoy additional support from free or subsidized parking. A driver traveling an

5. U.S. Bureau of Public Roads, "Federal Laws, Regulations, and Other Material Relating to Highways" (1960; processed), pp. 5, 12, 21.

urban expressway during the rush hour pays the same federal and state gasoline tax per mile as a motorist on a rural road. Since much of the capacity of new expressways was built primarily to accommodate traffic in the peak hour, a uniform highway charge means that peak-hour users are subsidized by other drivers. If the roughly 40 percent of urban traffic that moves in rush hours were charged incremental costs that were 20 percent above basic system costs, the charge for road users in the rush hour should be 50 percent higher than it is now. In addition, urban motorists are avoiding the social costs of air pollution, accidents, and the noise, nuisance, and undesirable aesthetic effects attributable to motor vehicles; the community as a whole is called upon to pay part of these social costs. It has been estimated, for example, that every motorist driving into the central business district of New York during rush hours in 1972 was costing the city $500 a year. Motorists were paying another $180 million annually in extra costs to operate their vehicles in rush-hour congestion.[6]

Some of the external costs not paid by the motorist are now being internalized in the antipollution and safety devices included in the price of a car. But there will continue to be a sizable gap between the cost and price of an automobile ride as long as parking is subsidized. Free or subsidized parking in the company garage is a fringe benefit in lieu of salary that favors automobile owners over those without automobiles. The amount of subsidy often exceeds what nondriving employees pay to ride the bus. For automobile users who are not favored by a free parking bonus where they work, free parking at the curb may confer a municipal bonus. How much this amounts to can be judged by the difference between the parking charge at the curb and the charge for parking in an adjacent lot. If curb parking is permitted without charge and parking on an adjacent lot is $2.00 per day, the total subsidy for 250 working days a year is $500 per driver.

Transit fares, too, are distorted by both subsidy and perverse pricing policies, though to a lesser degree perhaps than in the case of the automobile. Rapid transit riders do not pay the costs associated with the construction of the system and generally benefit from an operating subsidy as well. Fare structures usually subsidize the long haul at the expense of the short haul, and there is rarely any effort to charge more for costly peak-hour traffic and less for the off-peak ride when much of the capacity of the transit system is unused.

Charging the motorist the full costs of driving in cities has been talked

6. Harry Schwartz, "Manhattan without Cars?" *New York Affairs*, vol. 1, no. 1 (1973), p. 48.

about for a long time, but the political odds against it are high. There have been some recent successes in limiting free or subsidized parking on the streets, however, and it is possible that electronic billing or special license plates to cover the cost of driving in central areas during the rush hour might be introduced in some cities.

If the total costs of city driving are not paid by the motorist, the transit rider might be further subsidized or provided with free public transportation to compensate. If this were to result in a shift from auto to transit sufficient to decongest the streets, even free transit might permit a net saving in total urban transportation costs. In New York City, where a high proportion of commuters already depend on transit and where the cost of supplying service is high, the loss of revenue from eliminating fares would be high, the effects on street congestion minimal, and overcrowding of public carriers would be worsened. (Actually, a fare increase has recently been necessary to help alleviate the city's financial crisis.) But in cities where people depend principally on automobiles and where most transit is by bus, the cost of supplying free bus service might be moderate compared with the saving in reduced congestion. A net benefit seems to have been produced by free transit in a 105-square-block area of downtown Seattle. This service, which has been carrying 12,000 daily riders, has reduced the number of cars on the streets by 7 percent and is credited with increasing retail sales by an estimated $7 million over a 12-month period.[7]

Whether or to what extent transit should pay its way through fares is still debated on the grounds that excessively high fares will discourage riders (who will then drive and make things worse), while excessively low fares will not produce enough additional travel to generate the revenues needed to maintain good service. When the Metropolitan Atlanta Rapid Transit Authority (MARTA) reduced its 40-cent fare to 15 cents and dropped the 5-cent charge for transfers, the 62 percent decline in basic fare resulted in only a 21 percent increase in patronage by the end of the first year and, consequently, a heavy financial loss for the system. Nonetheless, some of the travel induced by the lower rate may have included that of people who previously could not afford to ride, and traffic shifting from automobiles may have helped to reduce street congestion. Thus the external benefits might have been worth the losses to the transit system. City officials, believing this to be the case, have allocated a portion of a special retail sales tax to MARTA to cover the deficit.[8] New York City's half-fare transit on Sundays and reduced evening fares are other

7. American Transit Association, *Passenger Transport*, vol. 32 (August 30, 1974), p. 3.
8. MARTA, *Annual Report, 1973*, pp. 2, 15.

examples of increased demand resulting from fare reduction, with consequent benefits to people without cars who are now better able to enjoy the social and recreational advantages of the city.

The principal reforms in transit pricing policy, however, may not be changes in the general fare level but in the internal structure of fares. A flat fare on many city transit systems means that a person traveling ten blocks pays the same as one going ten miles. One traveler may pay 35 cents a mile and another 3.5 cents. With the help of electronic ticketing (being introduced on the San Francisco and Washington rapid transit systems), it is possible to tailor the fare to the length of trip and therefore to charge the full cost of long hauls rather than permit cross subsidies from short-haul riders. With graduated fares it is possible that many who now walk or use their cars for short trips would pay a nominal amount to ride transit.

Transit demand is relatively price inelastic (since it is made up primarily of home-to-work travel), but loss of patronage does occur when fares go up, since some people will walk or stay home rather than pay the increase, and those with cars may elect to use them. Thus, while transit system revenues are increased by a rise in fares, pressures are exerted for more highway capacity, social costs are increased as a result of more congestion, and low-income families may find their mobility further restricted.

Generally an increase in fares is introduced without any increase in service. There has been no full test of consumer reactions to (1) an increase in transit fare accompanied by improvements in service, (2) a decrease in the fare accompanied by service improvements, or (3) either of the above with or without increased charges for driving. The current federal aid program may shed light on these possibilities as efforts are continued to improve transit and to hold down fares, with car and gasoline prices moving sharply up. But across-the-board increases in the cost of driving will not have the same effect as differential pricing of peak-hour travel. Whatever the effect of these pricing mixes might be, unless the federal aid program attempts to influence the pricing of both automobile and transit use, the effectiveness of capital grants in bringing about a shift from private to public transport will be limited.

A pricing policy that has not been tried is to assure that all urban transport—public and private—pays its full marginal cost. If both the motorist and the transit rider paid what it costs to accommodate them in the rush hours, both would pay more, and the motorist might be subject to the larger increase. The effect would be to reduce the total amount of transportation and to encourage the location of homes and workplaces on the basis of the resource costs required to get people moved. For motorists the effect would be that more would ride transit instead of driving or would use the car in off-peak hours. For transit patrons who could do so, there would be an incentive to ride off-peak, when marginal costs would be moderate and bargain fares would prevail. For all urban residents there would probably be higher standards of transport service, in part because reduced travel volumes would lessen congestion and in part because higher revenues would allow more funds to be used to make the service better, and taxpayers would not be saddled with the payment of transportation subsidies. By encouraging a closer relation between home and workplace, transportation prices based on costs would thus support land-use patterns in keeping with more vital and viable multi-function communities. Real estate investors now able through subsidized transport to benefit from one-purpose downtown office concentrations and high land values would face the prospect of lower land values and more dispersed concentrations of economic activity outside central business districts.[9]

The possibility of an overall strategy for pricing urban transportation has not been given much attention. It is easier to build expressways and rapid transit than to make some of the difficult political decisions that would permit an efficient and equitable use of the facilities already available.

Other Measures to Increase Efficiency

If the present multibillion dollar investment in roads and vehicles is to be used effectively to meet the transportation needs of the city, pricing policies must be accompanied by good traffic management to speed the movement of vehicles and reduce congestion. Among the more promising measures are the designation of streets or traffic lanes for buses only, the encouragement of car pools, the staggering of work schedules, the construction of fringe parking facilities at suburban transit stations, and the more widespread use of taxis and group-riding taxis. The benefits of such approaches are their low cost in relation to potential results.

In most cities the availability of free parking on the streets encourages automobile use. In New York half the cars driven into the central business district park free—most of them illegally.[10] One remedy is to strictly enforce a ban on street parking. Another is to establish vehicle-free zones or to ban cars from certain streets that could be converted to pedestrian shopping malls.

9. See Dick Netzer, "The Case against Low Subway Fares," *New York Affairs*, vol. 1, no. 3 (1974), pp. 14–25.

10. Schwartz, "Manhattan without Cars?" p. 50.

Many cities in Europe have created car-free shopping streets, which have reduced the volume of automobile traffic, increased dependence on walking, and encouraged the use of transit.

The carrying capacity of the taxi could also be greatly increased, both by enlarging the fleet and by group riding. Taxis are now limited in number in most cities in order to maintain high fares, and regulations barring entry into the business need to be relaxed. If taxis could operate as part of the public transit system and provide group-riding services, they would make a major contribution to improved transportation efficiency.

Jitney operations were once popular in the United States, but the transit industry reacted by promoting legislation to restrict these operations, and many of the restrictions still stand in the way of expanding taxi use.[11] Federal aid presents an opportunity to finance integrated bus-taxi systems to provide a total door-to-door service, with public automobiles substituting for private automobiles in areas of heavy congestion.

The extent to which low-cost traffic improvement programs have been tried to date is not impressive. In 1972 only three urban areas were considering the deregulation of taxicabs to provide more service of this kind, four were considering banning private cars from central business districts, and five were reserving lanes for buses. Changes in pricing policy were not being adopted to any large extent; no city was increasing bridge and tunnel tolls in rush hours, only 5 were reducing transit fares in off-peak periods, and 17 were increasing daytime parking rates in the central business district. Some staggering of work hours was reported in 36 urban areas, but there were few comprehensive plans, and car pools were being encouraged to some degree in 24 cities.[12]

Car-pooling is potentially a major means of putting unused transport capacity to work. There could be a 25 percent reduction in the number of cars used for the work trip if average load factors were increased from 1.5 persons per vehicle to 2.[13]

11. Arthur Saltzman and Richard J. Solomon, "Jitney Operations in the United States," *Highway Research Record,* no. 449 (Washington, D.C.: Highway Research Board, National Research Council, 1973), p. 63.

12. Information in this paragraph is from U.S. Department of Transportation, "1974 National Transportation Report" (Government Printing Office, 1974; processed), p. V-12.

13. See ibid., pp. V-17, V-18. In Minneapolis the use of van pools or minibuses for commuter service to large employment centers has reduced automobile use and the amount of land dedicated to parking. Passengers are picked up at, and delivered to, their houses. The driver, who is also a plant employee, takes the van home at night, rides free, and is encouraged to maintain a full load by being permitted to pocket the passengers' monthly fares.

An important possibility for increased transport efficiency also lies in reducing peak traffic requirements by spreading demand over a longer period of time. The gradual reduction in total hours worked per employee leaves more leeway for staggering arrivals and departures. Many occupations are becoming task oriented rather than time oriented, and where teamwork and consultation or supervision are unnecessary, a wider variety of workday schedules could overcome the peaking conditions that result when everyone heads for the same places at the same time.

A number of firms are experimenting with a four-day week, and some with a three-day week and two shifts in an effort to keep expensive equipment operating more hours of the day and more days of the week. A four-day week of nine hours per day with staggered days of work for each 20 percent of the work force (some on the job Monday through Thursday, others Tuesday through Friday or Friday through Wednesday) would reduce travel miles and fuel consumption by 20 percent. Transit would benefit by a reduction in the number of buses required, or service could be improved by an increase in the availability of seating.

A recent study of flexible working hours (now widely in use in European countries) indicates that this relatively new approach to work schedules in the United States has won the approval of workers, reduced absenteeism, and increased productivity. Of the 59 flexible-hour plans studied, none has reverted to rigid work hours. Under one plan the employee chooses his own hours, within a range established by the employer, and adheres to them each day. Thus all workers may be required to be present from 10 A.M. but may start as early as 7 A.M. and leave as late as 6 P.M. But the most common system permits day-to-day variations in the schedule of individual workers, as long as a specified number of hours are worked per week. Of the 40 firms using this "flexitime" plan, 18 reported increased productivity, none a decrease in productivity. Thirty-four firms reported a decrease in tardiness and 22 a decline in absenteeism.[14]

The obvious advantages to employees on a flexitime work schedule is that they can time their work according to how they feel and in conformity to household duties, outside appointments, and social and recreational activities. From the standpoint of the community, flexitime means a spreading of commuter hours, and if widely adopted could mean significant reductions in the need for highway and transit capacity.

In summary, there are many ways to increase the effectiveness of urban

14. "Hours of Work When Workers Can Choose," a study financed by the Business and Professional Women's Foundation, reported in the *New York Times,* July 7, 1975.

transport facilities, and if federal aid were to be made contingent on an all-out effort to do so, transportation conditions in urban areas could be quickly improved without a large commitment of resources. The situation may now be favorable for the acceptance of such a strategy in view of the rising cost of energy and the necessity for traffic restraints to meet clean air requirements. Yet measures to increase efficiency are generally uninspiring, restrictive, and politically distasteful, and without some degree of compulsion, efforts along these lines will continue to be resisted.

5

Integrating Transportation and Urban Development

The effectiveness of transportation policy decisions will depend in turn on policies governing the location of urban activities and the development of urban land. Urban sections of the Interstate Highway System are overloaded in rush hour, and subway systems are typically jammed beyond peak-hour capacity shortly after they open. Wherever such facilities attract new business enterprises along their routes, they often generate more traffic than they were designed to handle. Improved transportation will also result in higher urban densities, the removal of residential land uses from the central city, and further separation of home and work. Transport-induced decisions to relocate that make sense individually turn out to be socially disastrous when multiplied by large numbers. Without greater consistency between the building of transport capacity and the location and density of economic activity, the gap between transport supply and demand will persist.

The Demand Side of Transportation Problems

The limitations of conventional approaches to solving urban transportation problems stem from the institutions that deal with these problems. Solving transportation problems is not simply a matter of supplying capacity and therefore should not be the sole responsibility of agencies performing this function. In urban areas transportation problems are influenced by patterns of land occupancy, by the kinds of traffic generators allowed in congested areas, and by the condition of the environment of center cities. If transportation is to be manageable, jobs and services must be convenient to housing, the environment must be more satisfying than it generally is, and land-use patterns must be developed that create viable routes for public transit. It is not suggested that transportation agencies should be responsible for the demand side of the transportation problem but only that they form alliances with those that are.

41

Consumers make personal choices regarding housing, jobs, and transportation based on trade-offs that will give them less expensive housing for more costly transportation, or conversely, less commuting at the cost of less housing space and less recreation. They see transportation as only one element in the total system of activity in which they are engaged as members of the urban community, and they base their decisions on the mix that best suits their life-styles. In their daily lives people are able to relate transport choices to goals and living preferences, and governments should be capable of doing likewise.

Government is in no position to do this because of the way transportation developed. Each separate technology has been introduced at a different period of time, and each has gained a foothold by having its own institutional arrangements for survival. For many years the focus was on rural transportation and on creating traffic, not on managing it, let alone reducing it. Later, the extension of public interest beyond rural and intercity transport to urban transport called for a reorientation that has never taken place. The intercity transport task is to get from one fixed point to another, but in urban areas the patterns of land use are subject to manipulation. Urban transportation problems can thus be mitigated by the location of people and their activities, but departments of transportation, transit agencies, and highway departments have no power to make such decisions.

Accordingly, transportation has always been viewed as a matter of providing whatever capacity is needed, but without any constraints on demand this process has perpetuated shortages, regardless of the technology or resources used. Los Angeles and New York, one dependent on cars and the other transit oriented, are both victims of congestion in spite of extremely large transportation investments. The Los Angeles-Long Beach metropolitan area, with almost 4 million automobiles, 20,000 miles of streets, and 423 miles of freeways, has been considering an $8 billion to $10 billion rapid transit system to decongest the traffic. New York, which accounts for some 80 percent of all U.S. rapid transit passengers, also finds congestion at intolerable levels.[1] Metropolitan growth has responded to the increase in transport capacity with an over-concentration of offices, inadequate provision for close-in housing and amenities, and a lack of suburban jobs and services. As a result the volume of travel continues to increase more rapidly than new expressways and subways can be built. In both New York and Los Angeles, public policy has been based on the

1. Motor Vehicle Manufacturers Association of the U.S., *1975 Automobile Facts and Figures* (Detroit: MVMA, n.d.), p. 23; American Institute of Planners and MVMA, *Urban Transportation Factbook* (Detroit: MVMA, 1974), pp. I-28, I-29; and *Railway Age,* vol. 176 (October 13, 1975), p. 26.

false premise that more and better highways and faster trains can compensate for the disorganization of metropolitan life.

In earlier times transportation determined the nature of urban settlements because transportation was a constraint on development: the population of urban settlements was no larger than could be supplied and fed by the transport system. Most workers walked to their jobs, the radius of the city was short, and the area was small. Cities later grew larger as modern sewer and transport systems permitted, and they spread farther as railways, transit, and the motor vehicle extended the radius of the urban area. Today transportation has the capability of supporting any conceivable size or shape of city, but the urban community can no longer afford to settle for growth patterns merely because technology happens to make them possible. Urbanites must decide what kinds of communities they want to live in and then must use transportation technology to help achieve them. Otherwise no amount of transportation will solve the transportation problem.

It is this concept that is being introduced in planned communities and large urban redevelopment projects that are attempting to overcome congestion and inaccessibility by mixtures of land uses. These communities and projects seek to avoid functional overspecialization—the downtown office center that has no housing and is deserted at night, the dormitory suburb that is partially deserted in the daytime, and the all-slum area where everybody is poor. The Housing and Urban Development Act of 1970 provided support for such planned urban growth by encouraging "well-planned, diversified, economically sound new communities," including center city renewal areas.[2] Federal assistance was made available for projects that furnished an economically viable alternative to disorderly growth, that would preserve or enhance the natural and urban environment, and that could provide good living conditions, diversified land use patterns, and shelter for low- and moderate-income families.[3]

Solving Transportation Problems by Urban Design

Under the new-communities program, there has been only one effort to reverse the decline of an inner city, but it has demonstrated the key role of transportation in urban redevelopment. Cedar-Riverside is a new city for 30,000 people within walking distance of downtown Minneapolis and adjacent to the University of Minnesota. Part of the community's transportation problem may be solved before it arises, since many of the daily trips taken by

2. 84 Stat. 1794.
3. See Housing and Urban Development Act of 1970, S. Rep. 91-1216, 91 Cong. 2 sess. (1970), pp. 59-60.

Cedar-Riverside residents will be on foot on a system of pedestrian walkways that will link all major portions of the community. Some of these walkways pass through buildings and courtyards to provide pedestrians circulation at second-floor level. By the time Cedar-Riverside is completed, about 40 percent of the existing street mileage may be eliminated; land already vacated by street abandonments is being used to far greater advantage as sites for housing and recreation. Repetitive daily trips will also be reduced in volume and length because each neighborhood will be equipped with its own facilities for convenience shopping, health-care delivery, day-care services, and recreation.

Unfortunately, some excellent plans to solve transportation problems by urban design have been defeated or impeded by economic conditions, public or political resistance, or a combination of all three. Two such plans in particular are worth mentioning because they offer interesting guidelines for future redevelopment programs. One concerns Staten Island, New York; the other, Hartford, Connecticut.

Projections for Staten Island indicated that between 1970 and the end of the century 250,000 more people would settle in South Richmond, a community of 10,000 acres that is cut up into thousands of small parcels of land and that will inevitably turn out to be overcrowded, lacking in amenities, and short of transportation, jobs, and nearly everything else. To avoid this situation, an alternative was proposed—a planned city of 450,000 people, with a pedestrian-oriented town center, employment in industrial parks and commercial centers, and a series of separate neighborhood clusters delineated by highway and park systems, each with its own school, shopping, and recreation within a three- or four-minute walk for everyone. Internal transit was to connect the city center to town and neighborhood centers, while transport to the other boroughs of New York City was to be supplied by a tie-in to the subway. Instead of 30 percent of the area being devoted to streets, as at present, the alternative plan would have reduced street mileage to only 16 percent of the land area. Many trips by automobile would have been eliminated by the clustering of houses, schools, shopping, and recreation. If it had been accepted, this plan for South Richmond would have made the most of the possibilities that a combined federal aid program for transportation and urban development could promote. But the proposal was rejected by the state legislature because of opposition to the sizable amount of land that would have to be condemned and because of various political factors.[4]

4. See The Rouse Company, *A Report to the City of New York: An Analysis of Development Trends and Projections and Recommendations for a New City in South Richmond* (Rouse, 1970).

In Hartford a similar effort called for redeveloping 50 percent of the entire city and 75 percent of its commercial properties. Neighborhoods of about 10,000 people each were to be redesigned to overcome environmental decay and to provide good housing near work, vocational training and day-care centers, shops, clinics, community meeting places, and easy access to recreation. Although this program has been hard hit by a depressed economy and unemployment, the physical and economic models of the Hartford redevelopment process indicate that the public investments to achieve these superior facilities could provide enough revenue through land sales, government grants, and taxes to more than repay the entire investment over a 20-year period.[5]

Since redevelopment plans are so vulnerable to alteration or abandonment because of social, economic, and political factors, their possibilities for cost savings, including transportation and other infrastructure and service costs, have thus far lacked any large-scale practical demonstration in the United States. But these possibilities have been explored in a study in which models of alternative community designs show that unplanned communities are much more costly to build, operate, and provide with transportation than are communities of clustered housing within easy reach of service and recreational centers.[6] Two hypothetical areas were compared. Each covered 6,000 acres and had been designed for 10,000 dwelling units. One, in which all the land had been developed, was a typical suburban area with low-density sprawl and conventional single houses. The other was a planned suburb with half the land left vacant for recreation and most of the 10,000 dwelling units in town houses and apartments. The unplanned community would have to invest 65 percent more capital in roads, would use twice as much gasoline, and would pay higher costs for house construction, water use, sewage facilities, and electricity.

The best practical examples of planned cities that have been deliberately designed to provide more convenient, attractive, and resource-conserving communities are being built abroad. They include Great Britain's 28 new towns, the satellite cities around Paris and Singapore, and Mexico's Cuautitlan Izcalli, which will accommodate over a million and a half people. These and many other planned communities throughout the world[7] are experimenting with

5. American City Corporation, *The Greater Hartford Process* (Hartford: Greater Hartford Process, Inc., 1972).

6. Real Estate Research Corporation, *The Costs of Sprawl,* prepared for the Council on Environmental Quality, the Department of Housing and Urban Development, and the Environmental Protection Agency (Government Printing Office, 1974).

7. Among them are Brasilia, Brazil; Makati, Philippines; Shah Alam, Malaysia; and Tema, Ghana.

varying degrees of success to achieve urban designs that will help overcome the congestion and difficulty of access that typify the conventional planless metropolis.

Transportation and Design Innovations

A new potential for finding the solution of urban transportation and living problems through urban design may lie in combining federal redevelopment efforts with the new federal initiatives in metropolitan transportation. Often half the available space in central cities is devoted to streets, expressways, and parking, posing a formidable barrier to a better environment. Dedicating so much of the city to streets and parking lots means spreading the area thin, destroying its attractiveness, making good public transit impossible, and transforming the center into storage space for automobiles. The substitution of public transit or walking for the automobile in some parts of central areas could completely transform the environment and alter the character of communities and neighborhoods.

The possibility of improving the circulation of people in cities, of insulating people from cars, and of decongesting city streets with minimum capital investment is illustrated by Minneapolis. In the downtown area a pedestrian transportation network of 60 "covered bridges" is being provided at second-story level to connect the buildings in the central business district. On these climate-controlled, carpeted, and glass-walled skyways one can move around the entire downtown area on foot, protected from the weather, and find easily accessible shops and restaurants at the skyway level within the interconnected buildings. There is a large indoor terminal, and a multistoried glass-covered plaza serves as a focal point in the walkway system. Outside, the main shopping street has become a mall barred to automobiles, with landscaped walkways for shoppers and bus lanes in the center.[8]

The possibility of applying these ideas to other cities on a large scale by using buses on existing streets to serve auto-free areas can be seen by analogy in the operation of bus services on the campus of Michigan State University. The presence of automobiles on this campus for 40,000 students was creating so many parking difficulties, traffic tie-ups, and environmental problems that the decision was made to restrict the use of cars and to provide parking in peripheral lots, with a bus system operated by the university to take the place of private transportation. Students who use the service buy quarterly passes

8. See William Marlin, *Christian Science Monitor,* February 15, 1974.

and take more than 5 million bus rides a year.[9] The operation of a bus system in an activity center is different from ordinary transit service since it involves not just moving people but carrying out the function for which the complex was designed, in this case education. Ready access to the widely separated facilities on campus for all students was one aim. Another was to encourage living on the campus by making it easy to get from dormitory to classroom. It was worth subsidizing a bus operation if the subsidy was less than the rental income of students who would otherwise have left the dormitories to find more convenient quarters elsewhere. Since a university, like the downtown area of a city, has more important use for its land than parking lots, major gains were realized from banning cars and providing good public transit through changes in land use and environment.

The environment of old cities might be completely transformed if grant money available through the Department of Transportation were to be used in conjunction with urban redevelopment to create more livable and attractive communities. The possibilities include the redesign, landscaping, and lighting of the main streets and sidewalks, the use of streets as buffers to protect residential areas, the vacating of unnecessary streets to create superblocks and to release land for other uses, the creation of pedestrian malls, the construction of community-wide walkway systems, and the removal of utility poles and wires from the public ways. Federal aid for urban transportation should be used to promote the redevelopment of cities and to enhance the urban environment, while urban redevelopment should be a means of alleviating transportation problems. The highway and transit resources of the federal government should be combined with housing, health, education, water, sewer, and other federal programs in urban areas. Instead of calling off the program for new communities, the time has arrived for their creation in old communities. New-town principles also apply to suburbs, which could avoid the environmental destruction and waste of land, energy, and other resources that result from failure to plan suburban growth to create more desirable living and working conditions.

Steps are under way, however, to help bring about a more comprehensive urban planning process. The Department of Transportation is now making both highway and transit projects contingent on the same processes for assuring that transportation developments are part of a community plan. Transportation improvement programs in urbanized areas must be updated annually

9. Frank W. Davis, Jr., "Bus Transit System for a Major Activity Center," *Highway Research Record,* no. 449 (Washington, D.C.: National Research Council, Highway Research Board, 1973), pp. 34-35.

by a metropolitan planning agency designated by the governor of each state to assure that "individual transit and highway projects and programs are consistent with the long-range goals for regional development."[10]

A more basic solution lies in the creation of a Department of Community Development, which President Nixon proposed to Congress in 1971. By consolidating programs of housing, transportation, and urban services in one department, the stage would be set for a total attack on urban blight. Federal efforts affecting the city would be consolidated in the same way that city-building corporations pool resources for community building and renewal.

An effective integration of transport and urban development also calls for institutional innovations at the local level. The much-troubled New York State Urban Development Corporation (UDC) exemplifies such an innovation. In 1968 this first public city-building corporation was given responsibility for all aspects of urban development and redevelopment, from land acquisition to the construction of housing and the supply of community facilities and services. Until it recently came upon hard times, UDC could call on government bureaus and private contractors to participate in carrying out the work plans for which the corporation and its citizen advisory groups are responsible. This integrating process enabled transportation facilities to help create desired patterns of urban development and focused community development on the need to avoid unreasonable transportation requirements. Unfortunately, most of this work is now at a standstill because UDC is in serious difficulties as a result of a default on obligations in 1975 brought about by a combination of circumstances, including the moratorium on federal housing assistance and the fact that UDC's bonds lacked the full backing of the state. But a good example of what this arrangement can accomplish is the new town being built by a subsidiary of UDC on Roosevelt Island in the East River opposite the United Nations. On this narrow two-mile-long island, a completely auto-free community for 18,000 people is under construction. All cars will be left in a multistory garage at one end of the island, and the only transportation along the main pedestrian mall will be by minibus. Roosevelt Island will contain apartments, town houses, offices, shops, and schools in an environment designed to take maximum advantage of a unique waterfront location.

The federal government took a major step toward integrating transportation and urban development in the Housing and Community Development Act of 1974. This legislation consolidated several categorical aid programs into a single program to be supported by block grants for community development.

10. *Federal Register,* vol. 39 (November 8, 1974), pt. 1, p. 39667.

The purpose is to develop viable communities with good housing, a suitable living environment, and expanded economic opportunities. The act stipulates that $8.4 billion of federal funds may be used during the three years 1975-77 for this purpose, with no requirements for local matching. Applications from metropolitan cities and urban counties are required for federal approval and must consist of a three-year plan for meeting community development needs, eliminating slums, improving community facilities, and expanding the community's housing stock.

The permissible use of funds under the act includes the same kinds of activities provided for in the programs that were superseded. These include land acquisition, public works construction, building demolition, public services, code enforcement, the rehabilitation of buildings, and the provision of open space, recreation, streets, malls, and walkways. The distribution of funds to cities of 50,000 and over is based on a formula that includes population, the extent of overcrowded housing, and the degree of poverty.

The program as it now stands does not incorporate federal aid for urban transportation. This omission should be corrected—initially through cooperation between the Department of Housing and Urban Development and the Department of Transportation and eventually through a Department of Community Development—for the task is clearly to combine transportation and urban development in a total systems approach to the interrelated problems of urban communities. At the local level the need for an integrated approach might best be satisfied by the creation of state urban development corporations and their local subsidiaries. Such agencies could pool resources and plan as well as carry out the work of integrated urban systems building.

6

Energy and Federal Aid Strategy

The urban future and the transportation systems best suited to serve it will be influenced by the outlook for energy. The United States, with 6 percent of the world's population, uses almost one-third of the total energy consumed in the world.[1] But uncertainty about the petroleum supply makes it unlikely that this country can continue to draw so heavily on this particular resource; in the long run other sources of power will undoubtedly be required. Are there acceptable public transportation substitutes for the automobile, or are we to look for an answer in changes affecting the motive power of the automobile itself? The debate over petroleum supplies has revolved around various restrictive measures that might be taken to cut fuel consumption, such as increased fuel taxes and prices or rationing. But less has been said about the positive measures that should be taken to ensure the continuation of essential transportation services.

Restrictions through Taxes or Rationing

A reduction in automobile use could be accomplished without sacrificing essential mobility. About 33 percent of the mileage driven is for social and recreational purposes, and this could readily be reduced. Less frequent trips to the store would cut back on shopping mileage that now accounts for 7 to 8 percent of all driving. Even travel to and from work, which is 34 percent of the total, could be reduced considerably through carpools, riding the bus, and in some cases moving closer to work.[2] With higher prices or increased taxes to discourage driving, car owners would have to decide how best to conserve

1. *A Time to Choose: America's Energy Future,* Final Report by the Energy Policy Project of the Ford Foundation (Ballinger, 1974), p. 5.
2. The statistics are from Motor Vehicle Manufacturers Association of the U.S., *1975 Automobile Facts and Figures* (Detroit: MVMA, n.d.), p. 41.

on mileage. For many trips walking or using the telephone would be additional options.

In addition to persuading motorists to cut down on unnecessary travel, a higher gasoline tax would offer the opportunity to deposit the resulting revenues in a transportation fund that could be used to help finance transit modernization and a research and development program for both new transit systems and changes in automobile propulsion. An extra tax on gasoline of 10 cents per gallon would produce $10 billion from the 100 billion gallons consumed annually by all motor vehicles.[3] Higher fuel prices that deter auto use, however, would have adverse effects on automobile sales and services and act as a depressant on suburban real estate, tourism, vacation resorts, and a wide assortment of auto-dependent industries. To reduce these consequences, a basic aim should be to make the automobile more efficient as well as to provide attractive public transportation alternatives. There is an obvious need for consistency in federal approaches to transportation, energy, and economic development.

An Energy-Efficient Automobile

According to studies of the Department of Transportation and the Environmental Protection Agency, it would be possible between now and 1980 to make changes in the fuel efficiency and in the mix of small and large cars that would increase the performance of passenger cars from an average of 14 miles per gallon (mpg) in 1974 to 22 mpg in 1980—an increase of almost 60 percent.[4]

An increase in miles per gallon has already been achieved in the 1975 models. U.S. car models in 1974 averaged 14 mpg; in 1975 they averaged 15.9 mpg, a 13.5 percent improvement.[5] The efficiency of individual cars can be further increased by weight reduction, reduced aerodynamic drag, improved engines, and better transmissions. Engine improvements and weight reduction offer the largest potentials for improvement.

The Energy Policy and Conservation Act of 1975 is designed to accelerate industry efforts to achieve greater fuel efficiency by imposing penalties on manufacturers who do not meet specified standards.[6] The act specifies that a

3. Ibid., p. 48.

4. "Potential for Motor Vehicle Fuel Economy Improvement," Report to the Congress, prepared by the U.S. Department of Transportation and the U.S. Environmental Protection Agency (1974; processed), p. 4.

5. Ibid.

6. Public Law 94-163, December 22, 1975.

minimum auto efficiency standard of 18 mpg should be achieved by new cars in 1978 and 20 mpg by the 1980 models, with subsequent levels of efficiency to be determined by the secretary of transportation. Penalties will be imposed on car manufacturers who fail to meet the standards.

From "scenarios" developed by the Department of Transportation, it is apparent that very large reductions in fuel consumption are possible through a combination of technical changes in the car and further changes in the size and weight composition of the fleet. Scenario C for 1980 (see table 6-1) indicates that a combination of weight reduction, reduced aerodynamic drag, and transmission improvements could bring about a 43 percent gain in miles per gallon in the 1980 models. According to scenario D, more gradual improvements in car efficiency plus a shift to smaller cars could increase miles per gallon 63 percent by the 1980 model year. By 1985 average miles per gallon could be 84 percent higher than in 1974, and automobiles actually could be consuming 7 billion gallons less than in 1980, despite an estimated annual 2.6 percent increase in driving as automobile ownership continued to grow. But along with an energy-efficient car, it will be necessary to create a more energy-efficient transportation system, and it is for this purpose that an integration of federal aid programs for highways and transit could prove highly effective.

Complementary Federal Aid Policies

Major improvements in the energy efficiency of urban transportation could be accomplished by measures previously discussed for achieving more effective traffic management and by inducements to shift from automobiles to public transit. Elements of a federal aid strategy for energy conservation might include the allocation of the $7.3 billion of federal capital assistance for transit in 1975-80 (discussed in chapter 2) to bus and taxi transportation rather than to rail rapid transit. The grounds for such a decision would be that rapid transit affects too few people and too few cities and takes too long to build. It might also be desirable to combine the $4 billion of formula aid for transit with highway aid for busways and bus lanes and the construction of bus shelters, turnouts, and automobile parking areas adjacent to transit stops. Staggering work schedules could provide an immediate increase in transit capacity and comfort, with emphasis on "flexitime" work schedules. The program might also supply group-riding taxi systems for downtown circulation and for pickup and delivery services in suburban areas, including feeder service for suburban buses.

Table 6-1. Scenarios to Reduce Automobile Gasoline Consumption by 1980 and by 1985

	Gain in miles per gallon over 1974 (percent)		Total gasoline consumption (billions of gallons)[b]	
Scenario[a]	*1980*	*1985*	*1980*	*1985*
A. Modest improvements	28	27	81	86
B. Gradual improvements through the 1980s	33	52	80	78
C. Maximum improvement by 1980	43	44	77	77
D. Scenario B plus shift to smaller cars	63	84	73	66

Source: "Potential for Motor Vehicle Fuel Economy Improvement," Report to the Congress, prepared by the U.S. Department of Transportation and the U.S. Environmental Protection Agency (1974: processed), pp. 65, 66, 70.

a. Key to scenarios:

A. Optimized conventional engines, radial tires, slight weight reduction.

B. Weight reduction, substantial transmission improvements, and some aerodynamic drag reduction. Diesel engines for large cars phased in from 1981. Some stratified charge engines for smaller cars.

C. Rapid weight and aerodynamic drag reduction and transmission improvements, but no diesel or stratified charge engines.

D. Same as B with 1980 sales mix of 10 percent large cars, 50 percent intermediate, and 40 percent subcompact.

b. Assuming a 2.6 percent increase in driving per year.

Other longer-range measures could be taken to conserve energy in intercity public transportation. The railroads could expand piggyback operations for automobiles on intercity trips. An auto train carrying 100 automobiles and 200 passengers at 70 miles an hour could achieve an energy efficiency of 50 mpg per car.[7] The expansion of intercity bus travel and improved high-speed passenger trains are additional possibilities that would permit increased mobility at minimum petroleum requirements. Fuel consumption for the movement of goods by truck could be reduced by deregulation (to reduce empty mileage and circuitous routing), by the expansion of piggyback operations, and by the relocation of terminals and the consolidation of pick-up and delivery services. A national policy aimed at improving intermediate-distance rail travel on heavily traveled routes would extend to rail rights-of-way the kind of federal support now provided for highway, air, and water transport.

A number of estimates have been made of the total fuel savings possible through conservation measures and energy-saving equipment. The National Academy of Engineering has estimated that in 1985 a combination of lower

7. Richard A. Rice, "Toward More Transportation with Less Energy," *Technology Review,* vol. 76 (February 1974), p. 46.

speeds, car-pooling, and smaller and more efficient cars would save 3 million barrels of fuel a day.[8] Another analysis concludes that "the United States could almost double its collective mobility volume over the next 25 years and use less oil and energy per year than at present."[9] Assumptions underlying this estimate include a reduction in intercity travel by automobile from the current 90 percent of the total to 70 percent and the limitation of intracity trips by conventional cars to about half the urban travel total. This would be accomplished by the use of small electric-powered vehicles—an alternative to the increased use of buses. Rail rapid transit is assumed to be limited to what could be accomplished by a $50 billion expansion program.

Even without technological breakthroughs, such as a satisfactory electric car, substantial reductions in petroleum consumption would be possible. The adoption of a four-day week, for example, would reduce the number of work trips by 20 percent. If half the nation's employees were to adopt such a four-day week, there would be a 10 percent reduction in home-to-work driving, or a 3.4 percent total reduction in automobile use (10 percent of the 34 percent of total car use accounted for by work trips). A reduction in the speed limit from 55 to 50 miles an hour would reduce gasoline consumption by perhaps 10 percent[10] and would probably affect half of all auto travel, most of it intercity. The resulting reduction in fuel requirements would be another 5 percent. Meanwhile the replacement of the automobile fleet with smaller and more fuel-efficient vehicles would be taking place gradually. If President Ford's proposed goal of a 40 percent increase in mileage per gallon is achieved in the 1980 models, another overall 10 percent fuel saving would be achieved in 1980.[11]

It is more difficult to assess the effect of the federal aid program on transit riding. If a 15 percent shift from automobile to transit were to take place between now and 1980, affecting the 50 million cars used daily for the work trip,[12] then about 5 million fewer cars would be used for commuting (15 percent of 50 million cars divided by an estimated 1.4 persons per vehicle). This

8. National Academy of Engineering, "U.S. Energy Prospects: An Engineering Viewpoint" (NAE, 1974; processed), p. 3.

9. Richard A. Rice, "Energy Efficiencies of the Transport Systems" (New York: Society of Automotive Engineers, 1973; processed), p. 11.

10. See ibid., p. 9.

11. See "The Economy," The President's Address Delivered before a Joint Session of the Congress, October 8, 1974, *Weekly Compilation of Presidential Documents,* vol. 10 (October 11, 1974), p. 1241. The 10 percent fuel saving is based on the assumption that half the fleet is replaced over the six-year period and that uniform progress is made toward the 40 percent goal in new car models each year.

12. *U.S. Department of Transportation News,* 108-74, December 13, 1974.

shift would result in a 5 percent reduction of fuel consumption. And if the federal goal of encouraging car-pooling by computer-assisted systems were to be successful—increasing load factors from 1.4 persons (the average in 1974) to only 1.6 persons per vehicle—total gasoline consumption would be reduced another 12 percent from 1974 levels.[13]

Altogether the effect of these measures in 1980 would be a 35 percent reduction in fuel consumption, assuming a fleet of stationary size. If the growth in the number of cars is assumed to be 2 percent a year,[14] the number of vehicles on the road would be 12.6 percent greater in 1980 than in 1974. In that case the fuel saving would be only about 30 percent.

The foregoing are conservative estimates of what could be accomplished if federal aid programs for highways and mass transit were made responsive to the need for conserving energy and if federal aid were combined with industry efforts to produce an energy-efficient automobile. A further long-term potential for energy conservation lies in successful programs of urban redevelopment that create energy-conserving cities.

Technological Innovations and Federal Research and Development

Other possibilities for energy conservation lie in the prospects of innovative public transit technology to provide substitutes for the automobile. Personal rapid transit and group-riding transit continue to be the subjects of research and development in many countries, notably France, Germany, the United States, and Japan. Considerable progress is being made toward a fully automated vehicle on an exclusive guideway that may carry anywhere from 2 to 100 people and may be used for shuttle services in major activity centers or, at some future date, for more complex systems operating over a wider urban area.[15]

One such system may be evolving from Airtrans, the "people mover" at the Dallas-Fort Worth airport. Although this $33 million system was shut down in late 1975 because of litigation over contracts, it had demonstrated

13. If 50 million cars are used when occupancy is 1.4 passengers, only 44 million would be required with a load factor of 1.6.

14. See Gerald Leach, "The Motor Car and Natural Resources" (Paris: Organisation for Economic Co-operation and Development, 1972; processed), p. 4.

15. See *Automated Guideway Transit: An Assessment of PRT and Other New Systems Including Supporting Panel Reports,* Prepared by the Office of Technology Assessment, U.S. Congress, for the Transportation Subcommittee of the Senate Committee on Appropriations (Government Printing Office, 1975).

its technical capabilities for two years. Fully automated and electrically pro-pelled, the system operates on a 13-mile concrete guideway that transports passengers, baggage, freight, employees, mail, and refuse to some 50 destina-tions. The 68 vehicles each carry 40 passengers. The concrete guideway, mostly at surface level, is an integral part of the airport itself.[16]

If a system of public transit similar to Airtrans were introduced in down-town centers, it might be possible to release large areas of street and parking space for other productive uses. Automobiles could be left outside the center, with remote parking provided as it is at the airport. The result would greatly improve the functioning of the downtown area, would provide ease of access throughout the area, and would release land for housing, green space, and recreation, all necessary to the creation of a living community rather than a daytime employment center.

In the new community of Fairlane in Dearborn, Michigan, the Ford Motor Company, sponsor of the development, decided several years ago that the automobile should be left outside in perimeter parking lots, with free public transit for quick service to the center. There were three possible methods of achieving these ends: buses on public streets, buses on exclusive bus lanes, or an elevated guideway with automated vehicles moving over it. The guideway system was preferred because of its low operating costs, higher speed, and ability to move through buildings to let passengers off within them. This type of automatically controlled transport system is based on automotive technol-ogy and operates on an elevated structure. The driverless rubber-tired vehicle carries 12 seated passengers and 12 standing. Developers of the new city found that this transport system would permit major cost advantages by eliminating thousands of parking spaces and releasing large areas of land that would otherwise be needed for streets.

This ambitious plan has been shelved, however, because investors in Fair-lane business activities preferred the automobile to a new and untried trans-port system.[17] Instead of a virtually car-free community with substantial guideway mileage, major reliance will be on automobiles, and a single guide-

16. See Thomas M. Sullivan and James E. Martin, "Airtrans Automated Transit at Dallas/Fort Worth Airport," *Traffic Engineering and Control*, vol. 15 (October 1973), pp. 285-87; and "Airtrans Comes to Dallas," *IRT Digest*, no. 19 (November-December 1973), pp. 26-29.

17. Confidence in the new system was not strengthened by events in Morgantown, West Virginia. There, the automated people mover on the campus of the University of West Virginia was so hurriedly designed that its operation (which began in late 1975) was delayed several years after construction and its costs eventually mushroomed to more than $64 million for 2.2 miles. See Office of Technology Assessment, *Automated Guideway Transit*, pp. 146-49.

way will be constructed from the shopping center to the hotel. This means that land in the new community must be made available for parking, and as a result, much of the economic justification for the people-mover system—that is, the saving of land for other uses—no longer applies.

Detroit is providing another illustration of the merits of auto-free zones for cities. The half-billion-dollar redevelopment project, Renaissance Center, is restoring the city's central waterfront with a hotel, office, apartment, and condominium complex. An automated people mover may be incorporated into the project to supply internal circulation and to connect Renaissance with the central business district and a proposed housing development to be created on the site of a lake-front railway yard.[18]

In some downtown areas it may be possible to provide shuttle transit services between buildings or sections of the city comparable to the shuttles now operating at the Tampa, Miami, and Seattle-Tacoma airports. As a substitute for both automobiles and conventional transit, these systems provide service from the terminal to boarding areas in automatic cars moving on a concrete guideway. At Tampa, the large rubber-tired cars can carry 125 passengers (all standing) at a top speed of 36 miles an hour. The capacity is 6,000 people per hour, which could be doubled by attaching a second car, and the trip takes 40 seconds. The cost of Tampa's 5,000-foot system was $5.6 million.[19] The use of this type of "horizontal elevator" in linear office and shopping districts with parking and long-haul transit facilities at either end might alleviate center city congestion, reduce energy costs, and make possible new land-use patterns freed from the constraints imposed by the automobile.

The unsatisfactory performance of present methods of mass transit emphasizes the need for new technology to provide more satisfactory solutions. Research and development in the Department of Transportation is now moving in the direction of supporting such innovation. The UMTA program commands some $30 million a year, of which $11.5 million is spent for new systems research, $15.3 million for conventional rail transport, and $3.6 million for bus research. An additional $7 million is spent for demonstration projects.[20]

Bus research is concerned with correcting the inadequacies of present

18. Information from the Renaissance Center staff and *Detroit Renaissance: A Three-Year Report* (Detroit Renaissance, Inc., n.d.).

19. Howard R. Ross Associates, "Perspective on PRT Systems for the Los Angeles Area," prepared for the Southern California Association of Governments (Menlo Park, Calif.: Howard R. Ross Associates, 1974; processed).

20. This information on research and development and that which follows is from tabulations and other material provided by the U.S. Department of Transportation.

equipment, which is frequently oversized, underpowered, noisy, uncomfortable, and difficult to enter and leave. The absence of major bus improvements over a period of some 15 years led the federal government to explore the possibilities of innovations to improve bus operating characteristics. Federal projects are aimed at designing a high-capacity bus to carry 75 or more seated passengers during rush hours and a small bus for light traffic routes.

For rail transit UMTA has supported the development of a rail car to improve passenger comfort and operating efficiency and an advanced passenger train that goes beyond current technology to achieve power conservation, improved riding qualities, and more economical maintenance. Vehicle testing is done at the Department of Transportation's 30,000-acre research facility near Pueblo, Colorado, where the new propulsion systems and advanced concepts are being developed.

New systems research is focusing on individualized public transport known as personal rapid transit (PRT). These systems consist of small vehicles for individuals or members of a group (four or six passengers) that travel nonstop on elevated or surface concrete guideways from any origin to any destination in the system selected by the rider. Loading and unloading are done off the regular line to avoid reducing system capacity because of vehicles stopped in stations. Service is available on demand 24 hours a day, speeds are equal to or above that of the automobile, there is no parking problem, and costs can be kept low because each vehicle can be used by many trip-takers rather than parked most of the time, as the automobile is.

A recent assessment of the state of PRT indicates that while progress has been limited thus far, the outlook is sufficiently promising to consider this a possible alternative to conventional mass transport in this century. Because of safety considerations, PRT systems are currently limited to fairly long headways between vehicles (10 to 20 seconds) and to speeds of about 30 miles per hour. Ten years hence headways could conceivably be reduced to two to four seconds, speeds increased to 45-60 miles per hour, and one-way capacities (with six-passenger cars) increased to about 10,000 people per hour.[21]

But there are still many technical problems to solve before automated guideway transit becomes a reality. The development of PRT systems would involve extensive new capital investment in guideways and might be limited to high-density clusters and central business districts rather than being introduced as an area-wide metropolitan transit solution. Little is known about the costs, performance, safety, and social acceptance of these systems, and there

21. See Howard R. Ross Associates, "Perspective on PRT Systems for the Los Angeles Area."

is a need for continuing efforts to assess the PRT experience to date, here and abroad, and to explore the possibilities of funding further technological development and the creation of prototypes. The concept of automated guideway transit for both passenger and freight movement in densely populated areas suggests important long-run possibilities for capital- and energy-efficient substitutes for both conventional rapid transit and the automobile.

Another area of research with important implications for future urban development patterns involves improved high-speed intercity public transportation for the intermediate ranges too short for efficient air transport and too long for the automobile. The so-called high-speed ground transportation research program sponsored by the federal government is an exploration of the possibilities of such substitutes for conventional railways. High-speed trains propelled by linear-induction electric motors at speeds of 150 to 300 miles per hour would derive their economy from the rapid turnaround of equipment and the consequent ability to reduce capital costs per passenger. A further potential of high-speed ground transport lies in the possibility of linking many moderate-sized cities in a single urban regional federation that could achieve economies of scale comparable to those of one large metropolis. While each community in the region would be largely self-sufficient, access to the whole region could be provided by guideway vehicles covering a distance of 100 miles or more in a half hour.

A primary responsibility of the federal government should be to conduct research and development to promote energy-conserving public transit substitutes for the automobile that offer sufficiently attractive and economical service to overcome the congestion and inequities of urban systems designed mainly for automobiles. The possibilities of integrating such technologies with innovative community design suggest the direction in which solutions to both living and moving in urban areas might be found.

For the time being, urban areas are heavily dependent on the family car, and the most urgent short-run goal for federal research and development efforts is the creation of a private vehicle that is less energy-consuming, less polluting, and less costly. These efforts should include contracts with private enterprise to create new propulsion systems for automobiles, new fuels, and improved automotive designs. The federal program has made some minor moves toward assisting in the development of battery-powered vehicles but for the most part has been lax in its efforts to assure energy-efficient private transportation.

7

Cost Implications of Alternative Federal Policies

The extent of the shift in federal aid from highways to mass transportation cannot be fully determined as yet. From the beginning of transit aid in 1964 until 1972, the volume of transit riding, which had been declining since the end of World War II, dropped by another billion and a half passengers, or 25 percent. But in 1973 the prolonged downward trend came to an end; in 1974 transit patronage increased 6 percent over the previous year and maintained this level during 1975.[1] The oil embargo that began in late 1973 and the subsequent sharp rise in the price of gasoline contributed to the increase in transit riders. The effect of the bus program is likely to give added impetus to transit patronage as the replacement of overaged bus equipment is completed and as new bus purchases result in further expansion of the fleet. There also may be added gains in transit riding as new rapid transit facilities come into full operation.

The financial fortunes of public transit have been less favorable since the aid program began. A moderate profit of $30 million for the industry as a whole in 1960 turned into a deficit of over $1 billion in 1974.[2] Part of the losses are the result of inflation and of public resistance to higher fares, but part can be attributed to the efforts of local governments to maintain services by purchasing private companies that would otherwise have ceased operations. There has also been a conscious acceptance of deficits in recognition of the essential public service provided by mass transportation and the high costs of alternative reliance on automobiles. These losses plus current estimates of new capital needs add up to sharply mounting transit bills for the future.

1. Transit data from American Public Transit Association, '74-'75 *Transit Fact Book* (Washington, D.C.: APTA, 1975), p. 17; and from the APTA statistical department.
2. APTA, '74-'75 *Transit Fact Book,* p. 12.

Future Urban Transportation Requirements

Capital expenditure requirements for transportation in the nation's urbanized areas over the period 1972-90 are estimated at $254 billion. Some $192 billion, or about three-quarters of the total, is for highways and $62 billion is for transit. Table 7-1 presents a breakdown of the transit expenditures. Average annual capital outlays for both highways and transit during the period are expected to be $14.1 billion. Additional outlays to cover the cost of highway operations and maintenance are expected to increase from $2.9 billion in 1971 to $4.6 billion in 1989. In 1989 transit deficits are expected to be at least $2.5 billion. The total public outlays projected for urban transportation may therefore be in the vicinity of $21 billion in 1989.[3]

Government projections put 1990 transit patronage at two and a half times present levels, or 14 billion riders per year. But transit's share of total passengers would remain where it is today, at about 6 percent.[4] These estimates lead to the uncomfortable conclusion that the very large outlays about to be made for transit, with major federal support, cannot be expected to alter the commitment of U.S. cities to the automobile to any appreciable extent.

The question is whether the anticipated annual expenditure of $21 billion of public funds for urban transportation by 1989 reflects a careful consideration of urban priorities and transportation alternatives. Should a larger proportion of transportation funds be spent for transit, or should there be a change in the allocation between bus and rail? Alternatively, should more attention be given to revising public policies to make the existing transport system and any further investments work more effectively? Is it defensible to allocate $21 billion of public funds annually to transportation, given the urgent problems of slums, blight, and disorderly growth that underlie many of the transportation problems of the cities?

More specifically, is it wise to allocate a total of $62 billion for public transit capital outlays over two decades only to wind up with the proportion of transit to total riding the same in 1990 as it is today? If the objectives are to reduce congestion, to save energy, to assist those who are without cars, and to enhance the urban environment, this program is apparently not going to deliver anything like the desired results. It is not enough for the nation simply

3. Amounts are in 1971 dollars and are from U.S. Department of Transportation, "1974 National Transportation Report" (Government Printing Office, 1974; processed), pp. III-18, V-7, V-10, V-21. As noted in chapter 2, the administrator of the Urban Mass Transportation Administration has estimated that the transit deficit could be as high as $4 billion in 1981.

4. U.S. Department of Transportation, "A Study of Urban Mass Transportation Needs and Financing" (Government Printing Office, 1974; processed), p. I-4.

Table 7-1. Projected Change in Vehicle Fleet and Route Miles and Capital Expenditures for Transit, 1972-90

Type of transit	Number of vehicles in fleet (thousands) 1972	Increase, 1972-90	Route miles (thousands) 1972	Increase, 1972-90	Capital expenditures between 1972 and 1990 Amount (billions of 1971 dollars)	Percentage of total
Bus	50,100	24,000	49,200	26,500[a]	8.2	13
Rail	10,600	7,500 ⎫	3,200	1,580[b]	41.0	67
Commuter rail	n.a.	700 ⎭		20	5.5	9
Other[c]	0	7,900	0	3,400	6.9	11
Total	60,700[d]	40,200	52,400	31,500	61.7	100

Sources: American Transit Association, *1974-75 Transit Fact Book* (Washington, D.C.: ATA, n.d.), p. 24; U.S. Department of Transportation, "A Study of Urban Mass Transportation Needs and Financing" (Government Printing Office, 1974; processed), pp. III-16, 18, 19, 21; and Department of Transportation, "1974 National Transportation Report" (Government Printing Office, 1974; processed), pp. V-7, 8. Figures are rounded.
  n.a. Not available.
  a. Includes 1,400 miles of new busways or exclusive bus lanes.
  b. Includes 1,200 miles in cities with no rail service at the present time (586 miles in Washington, Atlanta, Baltimore, Detroit, and Los Angeles and the remainder in small cities).
  c. Includes personal rapid transit, skybus, people movers, dial-a-ride, and similar systems.
  d. Does not include commuter rail figures, which are not available.

to spend more for urban transportation. What is needed is a strategy that links federal aid for highways and transit to the revision of transport management policies and that links this package in turn to energy conservation and the renewal of cities.

Alternative Strategies

There are several factors to be considered in arriving at an acceptable total strategy. One is how far and how fast we can move to design and produce an energy-efficient automobile. Another is the issue of rail rapid transit or bus. Still another is the extent to which the federal government will impose policy conditions on the recipients of transit and highway aid. And finally, the least understood issue concerns the relation of transportation to the rest of the urban system—how to mount an attack, not on transportation alone, but on the underlying urban conditions that generate the traffic that transportation systems are called upon to accommodate.

In arriving at an overall strategy, there are also important constraints that have to be taken into account. One is that people allocate a fairly stable percentage of household budgets for transportation and that further increases in this percentage brought about by inflation and energy costs cannot be sustained indefinitely. The other is that people also have fairly stable time budgets for their trips, and these also appear to be relatively unchangeable. These two constraints impose limits on what kinds of public policies will prove acceptable.

Since the mid-1920s, when the automobile first became popular, consumer outlays for transportation ranged between 10 and 13 percent of total consumer expenditures. Recently the rising prices of cars and petroleum have increased the pressures for a higher proportion of household outlays to be spent for transportation (13.6 percent in 1973).[5] The rising cost of food and shelter may create even greater pressures and force a decline in transportation outlays relative to the total. If so, reductions might be brought about by changes in the car itself (smaller and more durable models), by decreasing annual mileage through higher gasoline taxes, or by relinquishing second and third cars as alternative public transit services are improved and expanded. But as most forecasts of public transit riding indicate, the possibilities of any sizable increase in the ratio of public to private transport will not be easily accomplished. The percentage of consumer expenditures used for local public transit has been small and declining. If, however, transit spending were to be restored from its level of about a fifth of 1 percent of consumer expenditures in the 1970s to the 1 percent level of the 1930s, then an economy with total consumer outlays of a trillion dollars could provide $10 billion a year for urban public transit.

Riding transit, however, generally involves more trip time than driving a car, and given a 24-hour day, much of it devoted to working, eating, and sleeping, the average urban resident has limited time left to travel. If he is forced to shift from car to slower methods of transit he will forgo some trips that would otherwise have been taken in order to keep within his time budget. Thus automobile congestion can reduce total mobility and the advantages consumers seek to obtain through travel. The same can be said of any major shift to slower transit. The escape from these traps may be to live closer to daily destinations, to press for measures to reduce auto congestion, to improve the speed of transit, or to begin changing the nature of urban development patterns in ways that substitute accessibility for movement.

These are the difficult time-cost relationships that federal policy for trans-

5. J. Frederic Dewhurst and Associates, *America's Needs and Resources* (Twentieth Century Fund, 1955), pp. 990-92; and U.S. Department of Commerce, *Survey of Current Business,* various issues, table 2.5.

portation and urban development must in the end be capable of dealing with. They make clear the trade-offs involved in arriving at genuine improvements in mobility. Greater cost-effectiveness in urban transportation is a basic need, and the question is how to achieve it in a way that furthers community goals, conserves energy, promotes economic well-being, respects the constraints on consumer time and money, and recognizes the needs of those without cars. The range of policy choices is broad.

1. *Continue the present program, with the emphasis on rail rapid transit.*

The federal transit program and the urban transit programs projected by state and local governments allocate the major part of federal aid to rail systems. If this policy continues and the major part of the Urban Mass Transportation Administration's $8 billion fund for capital projects is used for new rail rapid transit, the money will not go far. Yet major cities now considering such systems include Los Angeles, Denver, Miami, Honolulu, and San Juan, among others. Thus large federal appropriations would be needed for these cities, as they were for San Francisco, Atlanta, Baltimore, and Washington.

If federal policy moved in this direction, it is not unlikely that some $50 billion of rapid transit funding might be sought from the federal government in the next few years and that an annual federal transit aid program of $5 billion might be required. Since a relatively small percentage of total trips would be accommodated by rapid transit (although a larger proportion of work trips), there would be little diminution of bus transport needs or of highway requirements for the automobile. Thus the total bill for capital investment, highway operations, and the payment of transit deficits may be greater than the high projections already contemplated.

On the other hand, the transportation benefits to be achieved by continuing to place emphasis on rapid transit would be substantial. It would be possible to improve the environment by getting traffic underground and to reduce trip times for those living and working close to rapid transit stations. With adequate patronage, there could also be a saving of energy. Moreover, a well-integrated rail and bus system might provide a comprehensive transit network that would persuade many families to forgo the use of their cars for work trips and eventually to give up the ownership of second and third cars.

It may be desirable to finance federal programs for rapid transit and energy conservation by a further tax on gasoline to discourage the use of the automobile. An additional tax of 10 cents a gallon could help finance urban redevelopment outlays of $10 billion a year, including improved transit. Such a tax would also help to compensate for the social costs of urban driving that are not covered now by motor vehicle tax payments, and applying the proceeds to the improvement of the cities would be a recognition of the social benefits of space-saving and energy-conserving urban redesign and public transit.

In view of the essential nature of much urban automobile travel, however, and the already high price of gasoline, the possibility of a less costly and more rewarding strategy needs to be considered.

2. Adopt a minimum-cost program with principal reliance on buses for transit and greater emphasis on traffic management and pricing policies.

An alternative federal policy would be to make more effective use of the already sizable transportation investment in urban areas and to focus on the expansion of public transit through relatively low-cost bus systems. This strategy would put the emphasis on traffic management, tax and pricing policies, flexible work schedules, and other measures designed to achieve greater efficiency.

Under current legislative authorizations, the federal government can exercise wide latitude in how it permits transit funds to be spent. Influence over the program can be exerted by conditions imposed on state and local governments in connection with both specific projects and the distribution of formula funds. The Department of Transportation requires each urbanized area to submit a general transportation plan as a condition for receiving formula grants, and this in itself will lead to the consideration of pricing and tax policies, traffic engineering solutions, preferential treatment for buses, expanded taxi services, staggered work hours, and other measures designed to make more efficient use of the existing system. By adding to mass transport capacity quickly, this low-cost bus-oriented program could help all cities simultaneously. Buses are also better able to meet the needs of low-income families and others who do not own an automobile. But most of the $8 billion of discretionary capital funds now available for transit is already committed to rail systems.

If there could be a concentration of capital on bus acquisition and a further use of highway money to facilitate transit, cities could provide better public transportation at relatively modest cost. The outlay necessary to provide the additional 24,000 buses estimated by state and local governments to be needed between 1972 and 1990 would be $1.5 billion, and the replacement of half the existing fleet by 1990 would cost another $1.5 billion. The federal share of the total cost would be $2.4 billion. Additional outlays for taxi and group-riding taxi systems and other capital needs might raise the federal outlay over the period ending in 1990 to $3 billion.

An effective low-cost transit program to ensure a higher proportion of urban travel by transit than the program now projected would also require highway funds to be used for systems of exclusive bus lanes and bus streets and for bus shelters, turnouts, and fringe parking for integrated auto-bus networks. Such a program could quickly improve the quality of transit service at a relatively modest cost and supply an energy-efficient substitute for automobile traffic in central cities. It would need to be accompanied by measures to step up the conversion of the automobile fleet to more energy-efficient vehicles.

The potential benefits of transport efficiency measures are substantial. If it were possible by better bus and taxi service and by automobile traffic restraints to effect a 20 percent nationwide reduction in auto use for the urban work trip, about 50 billion vehicle miles of automobile travel could be eliminated from the morning and evening rush hours. At out-of-pocket cost savings of 6 cents per vehicle mile, automobile operating costs would be reduced by $2.8 billion per year, and $2.3 billion more could be saved if 10 percent of multiple-car families gave up one car. The total savings of $5.1 billion would be reduced by the cost of moving 20 percent more people by public transit (estimating transit operating costs plus subsidies at $3 billion a year). This cost would be $600 million; thus net savings resulting from the assumed shift to public transit would be $4.5 billion, far more than the cost of the entire current federal aid program for public transit.[6] Added benefits would result from the reduction of congestion for both transit vehicles and automobiles.

Although this strategy would exclude new rapid transit systems, it is necessary for cities now served by rail systems to extend and renovate their facilities and to equip them with new rolling stock. About 20 percent of the 1,200 miles of new rapid transit lines in the transit program of state and local governments are additions to existing rail networks.[7] If federal aid were to be limited to present systems, rail transit outlays might be reduced to less than $1 billion a year. Bus purchases at the rate of 10,000 a year would require an additional $600 million. A minimum-cost highway program for the cities, postponing completion of the urban interstate system, would save $1.5 billion

6. Estimates are based on data in Motor Vehicle Manufacturers Association of the U.S., *1975 Automobile Facts and Figures* (Detroit: MVMA, n.d.), pp. 32, 41, 48; U.S. Bureau of the Census, *Statistical Abstract of the United States, 1974* (Government Printing Office, 1974), p. 39; L. L. Liston and R. W. Sherrer, "Cost of Operating an Automobile" (U.S. Department of Transportation, Federal Highway Administration, 1974; processed); and APTA, *'74-'75 Transit Fact Book,* pp. 12, 18.

7. Department of Transportation, "A Study of Urban Mass Transportation Needs and Financing," p. III-9.

a year. Capital costs for transit and urban highways could be held well below $3 billion a year, or half the current level of expenditure.

3. *Initiate a joint program for urban transportation and the environment in cooperation with the community development block grant program.*

As noted earlier, part of the traffic in urban areas can be attributed to journeys that are either an escape from poor urban environments or a necessity imposed by the disorderly physical layout of the city. Efforts to remedy these conditions through urban redevelopment and a more orderly process of suburbanization could reduce the length of home-to-work trips and eliminate some trips altogether. Transforming the cities could substitute access for mobility.

The solution of urban transportation problems, including energy conservation, depends as much on improving the cities as it does on improving transport operations. A pooling of transportation and community development funds could effect a mutually reinforcing combined program. Community development block grants (see chapter 5) would need to be increased substantially, and urban highway and transit money would need to be made an integral part of the program. The use of these funds, together with federal assistance for housing, would make it possible to focus federal resources on the problems of the urban environment that underlie the excessive traffic and poor accessibility of urban areas.

It might also be possible to provide supplemental financing for such a program by putting a tax on energy that would promote the development of energy-conserving communities. Housing, industry, lighting, heating, and transportation all offer substantial possibilities for energy savings and would be promoted if urban redevelopment were to be paid for through taxes that raised the cost of energy. The higher cost of driving resulting from a tax of 10 cents a gallon on gasoline would encourage housing and neighborhood rehabilitation in central cities, cause people to live closer to employment opportunities, reduce long commuting journeys, and promote a shift from automobile to bus. The proceeds of such a tax on gas could be credited to the funds available for community development block grants, as well as help pay the cost of mass transit assistance and energy research and development.

The potential savings from integrating transportation and urban redevelopment are impressive. If the average length of the home-to-work trip were reduced one mile each way for the 50 million automobiles used daily for commuting, total travel per year would be reduced by 25 billion vehicle miles for a saving of 1 million barrels of oil a week. More significant would be the possible reuse of land now devoted to streets, which would be vacated by the planned clustering of neighborhoods and commercial areas. Since a mile of typical city street contains about six acres of land, converting only 2 percent of the 500,000 miles of local streets in American cities to other purposes would release 60,000 acres.[8] If the average price of urban land is assumed to be $100,000 an acre, real estate worth $6 billion could be made available to help support the redevelopment effort.

Improvement of the urban environment plus better public transport service might make it possible for many people to do without a second car and for some city dwellers to give up car ownership altogether. The result would be substantial savings in transportation costs. If 10 million people were to give up their cars, reducing the total number of vehicles by 10 percent, there would be an annual saving of $15 billion—assuming a total cost of $1,500 for depreciation and operation per car per year. If, as a result, 15 million people used alternative bus and taxi service—assuming an average of 1.5 persons had been riding in each vehicle that was given up—added transit costs might be $400 a year per person, or $6 billion. Net savings would therefore be $9 billion. Reduced auto congestion in rush hours as a result of the shift to transit would mean further savings.

Weighing the Alternatives

The major alternatives outlined above are not mutually exclusive, and a mix of policies will probably find the most widespread support. Whichever direction is taken, a further responsibility of the federal government will be the development of new systems of public transportation and the assurance of more efficient urban automobiles. A percentage of the federal aid transport program should be allocated to the search for solutions, including propulsion methods, transport management systems, and methods of integrating transportation and community design.

Acceptable urban living conditions in the future suggest something more efficient than streets clogged with individually operated cars. An alternative might be planned clustering of urban activity, with built-in transport facilities that combine elevators with so-called people movers and personal rapid transit on guideways. The clusters might be interconnected by fast guideway trans-

8. For street area and mileage, see Motor Vehicle Manufacturers Association of the U.S., *1973/74 Automobile Facts and Figures* (Detroit: MVMA, n.d.), p. 46.

port, with the private car supplying energy-efficient local movement under conditions of moderate density. Urban vehicles are likely to be powered by electricity. High-speed ground transport may be the energy- and time-efficient way of journeying moderate distances between cities, with rental cars at destination. Or dual-mode systems may some day prove feasible—automobiles under guideway control in heavily traveled areas but driver-operated where densities are low.

Since smaller fuel-conserving cars for city service are less desirable for longer journeys, additional federal financing would be required for rail transportation to substitute for intercity auto trips. If modern high-speed rail services are to be supplied, including auto-train facilities, substantial public investment will be necessary to modernize roadbeds, construct guideways, and purchase rolling stock. A practical solution would be to provide basic rail or guideway facilities publicly, as highways, waterways, and airways are provided, with private railway companies leasing the public ways and paying user charges the same as private truckers, airlines, and water carriers do.

But more important than technology is the need to see the urban transportation problem as an integral part of the total urban problem. The current federal aid transportation program perpetuates the erroneous view that moving in cities can be treated independently of living in cities. Yet urban transportation problems are heavily affected by central city decay, the planless sprawl of the suburbs, and by poverty, crime, and racial tensions. The task is to address the total problem, making transportation part of a general strategy.

The isolation of transportation from other elements of the urban problem applies to energy. The issues of how to cope with petroleum costs and supplies have generally failed to focus on the many possibilities of reducing fuel consumption in the transport sector or on the importance to the economy of maintaining essential urban transportation services.

The overriding fact is that most urban areas of the United States are totally dependent on highway-oriented transportation, and in particular on the private automobile. The idea that there can be a return to rail transportation or other public transit on a scale that will make a decisive change in transport patterns is an illusion. Changes in urban transportation are more likely to come about by changes in urban communities themselves, and by shifts in urban activity and changes in urban life-styles. Meanwhile the task is to make effective use of the multibillion-dollar highway network that has already been created, largely through past federal aid programs, and to adopt appropriate policies to make the investment pay off, including maximum help for the millions of people who depend on public transit. Equity demands more effective public conveyances for those without cars, and both the condition of the environment and the need to conserve energy demand appropriate alternatives to driving.

A more energy-conserving urban transportation system is completely in line with what needs to be done to reduce congestion, improve equity, and revive the cities. Thus:

—The production of energy-efficient automobiles will now be furthered by new federal penalties to guarantee early compliance with strict efficiency standards.

—The efficient urban use of automobiles and highways should be promoted by appropriate tax, pricing, and traffic management policies.

—The promotion of effective public transit is necessary through a combination of expanded bus and taxi fleets, more extensive transit networks, more frequent service, subsidized fares, and the designation of street space for the exclusive use of public vehicles.

—More careful evaluation of new systems of conventional rail rapid transit is essential. These systems are unlikely to provide an economically acceptable alternative to the bus except on high-density routes in a limited number of cities. Buses and variations of the taxi can provide quicker and more economical solutions in keeping with the geography of the metropolitan area, the state of municipal finance, the transportation demands of the urban population, and the many other claims on urban resources. Restrictions on automobile use in heavily traveled areas should be imposed if necessary to increase the efficiency of motorized public transit.

—If the densities supported by rapid transit result in lower total costs of urban living and in higher urban productivity and satisfactions, and if the sum of these two exceeds transit investment and operating costs, the system may be warranted. But for most cities in the United States, plagued by the poverty of large segments of the population and by threats of municipal bankruptcy, conventional rail rapid transit is not likely to meet the test.

—In any case the compelling need is a national commitment to improve the conditions of urban living and to put the problems of moving in perspective. A reordering of national priorities calls for avoiding excessive investments in transportation and dedicating resources instead to the transformation of blighted urban areas and to more self-contained communities designed to reduce transportation needs and thus energy needs.